The

Hormone Decision

7

Questions

to Ask Yourself and
Your Doctor About
Hormone Replacement Therapy and
Other Options

LINDA LAUCELLA

Contemporary Books

Chicago New York San Francisco Lisbon London Madrid Mexico City
Milan New Delhi San Juan Seoul Singapore Sydney Toronto

The McGraw-Hill Companies

1 2 3 4 5 6 7 8 9 10 LBM/LBM 1 10 9 8 7 6 5 4 3 2

ISBN 0-07-141615-3

Interior design by Robert S. Tinnon Design

The information contained in this book is compiled from various sources and medical experts. It is intended only as a source of information for women making decisions about hormone replacement therapy. No medical point of view or preferred medical treatment is suggested or endorsed. The benefits or health risks associated with any medical treatment program depend on a woman's individual health profile and cannot be determined simply by reading this book. Every woman making decisions about her own health care and medical treatment needs to consult a health-care professional.

This book is printed on acid-free paper.

Contents

Foreword

On July 9, 2002, a study on hormone replacement (HRT) therapy conducted by the Women's Health Initiative study was stopped. This was the first major study of HRT to look at the risks and benefits of combined estrogen and progestin, the synthetic form of progesterone. The study involved healthy menopausal women and found an increased risk of invasive breast cancer and cardiovascular complications (heart attack or stroke). Today, the only thing the "experts" can agree on is that the HRT decision is highly individual and must be an informed decision, where all the possible risks and benefits of taking—or not taking—HRT are disclosed.

Women with a family history of breast cancer were never considered good HRT candidates. So for this group of women things have not changed. However, women who were considered at higher risk for heart disease due to family history or other risk factors, such as Type 2 diabetes, are now more confused than ever.

As a bioethicist and sociologist who specializes in women's health, and as the author of numerous books on women's health, I am alarmed but not surprised by the HRT study's findings. I have been questioning the medicalization and pathologizing of menopause for years, along with millions of women who have taken their health into their own hands, turning to natural forms of hormone replacement therapy through plant estrogens (phytoestrogens), natural hormone therapy (NRT) or natural progesterone therapy. For too long women have become fodder for experimental medicine without their genuine informed consent. But many women have discovered through diet, physical activity, herbal alternatives, and natural forms of progesterone and estrogen that they can take charge of their health once more.

The lessons learned from this HRT study are not new; we have lived through this story before. DES (diethylstilbestrol), the Dalkon Shield, and Phen/Fen are all examples from the same women's health narrative.

I frequently get questions at my Web site from browsers and readers who are worried about the "new facts of menopause." The answer I always give is this: the road to good health is paved through self-education. I strongly believe that medical jargon continues to be a barrier to women's health decisions.

In *The Hormone Decision*, Linda Laucella is one of the first informed journalists to address the questions and concerns so many of you have. This book not only presents the latest research on the risks and benefits of HRT but also helps you educate your own doctor about your personal needs and goals regarding your health after menopause.

M. Sara Rosenthal, Ph.D.
University of Toronto Joint Centre for Bioethics
Associate, University of Toronto Centre for Health Promotion
Author of *The Gynecological Sourcebook* and *The Breast Sourcebook;* Founder, www.sarahealth.com

Acknowledgments

This book has been a tremendous group effort. I am grateful for the assistance of all the production, design, marketing, and editorial staff at McGraw-Hill-Trade/Contemporary Books, especially my production editor Rena Copperman for working alongside me every step of this book, publisher Philip Ruppel, managing editor Marisa L'Heureux, cover designer LaShae Brigmon, copyeditor Linda Gorman, interior designer Bob Tinnon, assistant editor Mandy Huber, and my editor Judith McCarthy, who set this book in motion and charted its course. I would also like to extend a very special thanks to M. Sara Rosenthal for writing the foreword. It was a wonderful experience to see this team of people work together to create *The Hormone Decision.*

Introduction

In the past when a fifty-year-old patient complained to her physician that she was experiencing hot flashes and night sweats, mood swings and irritability, sleep disturbance, lack of energy, body aches and pains, reduced ability to concentrate, and loss of memory, her doctor would reach for a prescription pad. No question about it, hormone replacement therapy could ease a woman through the menopausal transition.

By that point the woman's doctor would have taken an extensive medical history (or updated the one he had on file for a preexisting patient), conducted various blood tests, and perhaps other medical tests, and would have known that the benefits of hormone replacement therapy outweighed the risks for this particular woman.

However, doctors have became more hesitant to reach for the prescription pad since July 2002, when the news was released that the definitive hormone replacement therapy study (conducted by the Women's Health Initiative [WHI] of the National Institutes of Health) was abruptly stopped because it was determined that the risks for those taking Prempro (the estrogen/progestin combination medication) were just too great for the study to continue for another three years as was planned. This was pretty scary news for women already "on" hormone replacement therapy (HRT), especially for those who had been taking it as a daily supplement for a long time, having gone through menopause years ago.

As soon as media attention focused on the terminated Women's Health Initiative (WHI) study (released in the *Journal of the American Medical Association*) involving 160,608 postmenopausal women between the ages of fifty and seventy-nine, doctor's offices were inundated with telephone calls from panicked women asking what they should do about taking their hormones. But before long it was revealed that beyond the startling fact the study had been stopped, two important conclusions reached during the study were the reasons it could not be continued. First, contrary to long-held conventional medical belief, the hormone combination found in Prempro does not actually help to prevent heart disease. Second, the breast cancer risk for women taking the hormones, which was already a serious factor for women who considered taking them, was slightly higher than expected. The final risks versus benefits results of the study were as follows: risks associated with taking HRT include increased incidence of breast cancer, heart disease, stroke, and blood clots; benefits of taking HRT are that in the short term it relieves menopausal transition discomfort and distress, and in the long term it appears to help prevent osteoporosis and colon cancer.

When the facts were looked at closely, it became clear that while the results of this study provide necessary information for all women who consider taking HRT, there are actually three separate and distinct categories of women who are potential candidates for various types of HRT: first, women experiencing life-altering symptoms from hormonal changes during their menopausal transition; second, women who may benefit from taking HRT after menopause, based on their health history; and third, women who have had hysterectomies and are taking estrogen alone (called unopposed estrogen, i.e. without progestins.)

Hormone "supplements" were introduced to the market during the late 1960s with an aggressive marketing campaign by drug manufacturer Wyeth Pharmaceuticals—supported by a very popular book, *Feminine Forever* (1966), written by Dr. Robert Wilson, a gynecologist—claiming that taking estrogen alone was as close as medical science had come to finding the elixir of youth for menopausal and postmenopausal women. Based on studies that have been conducted since that time, we now know that not only were those claims misguided, at best they were also dangerous for some women to believe.

Still, many women who began taking estrogen during that period of time continue to do so to this day. In fact, a separate part of the WHI study involving women who have had hysterectomies and are taking estrogen alone continues uninterrupted, with the definitive results not expected until 2005. Because that study was not stopped early, as was the estrogen/progestin study, it is assumed to be safe for women without a uterus to take unopposed estrogen, while considering their breast cancer, heart disease, stroke, and blood-clotting risks. But even those women are wondering if they should reassess their options.

Deciding whether to take HRT can be a complicated and bewildering experience for a woman. What started out being estrogen alone now includes different kinds of estrogen, progestins, natural progesterone, and testosterone in various combinations and dosages. Each hormone offers different health benefits and some are known to have health risks and side effects. Because of the newly released information about HRT, while women already taking it are trying to decide whether to continue, those who have not started taking it are more confused than ever about what choices to make.

How can this book help you make decisions about HRT and its benefits for your overall health? This guide combines the knowledge of experts from various aspects of women's health to explain what happens to your body during and after menopause, and suggests what HRT and natural health care choices you can make. Because I am not a health care professional, no preferred treatment program or medical point of view is expressed. Like you, I am a health care consumer looking for the most effective care I can find to maintain my current good health into the later years of life. The main difference between you and me is that it's my job, as a writer, to find the information about women's health care that you would like to know.

Let's begin by putting menopause into perspective: Menopause is not a disease that needs to be treated, although the hormonal changes during menopause can result in serious health problems later in life. It does not signal the end of your vitality, your sexuality, or your womanhood. Menopause is only one of a natural series of changes we undergo throughout our lives. Our first dramatic change of life was when we entered adulthood during puberty. Beginning at that time, we became aware of the constant ebb and flow of hormones within our bodies. Since then, we have learned to anticipate the complex series of pain and pleasure that results from living in a woman's body. During our thirties to mid-fifties, our ovaries slow down their production of hormones, we gradually enter our second dramatic change of life, and we need to understand that our bodies will operate differently.

Although the cessation of hormone production is gradual, the effects on our bodies are obvious to us. Not only do we feel different, but we begin to look different as well. Of course, that can make us fearful. Our first change of life, during puberty, was considered good. Despite the physical and emotional confusion we felt when our ovaries began to produce hormones, we were rewarded with the enhanced physical appearance of becoming a woman and the ability to produce children. But this second change of life called menopause is perceived differently. At times it can feel very mysterious and confusing to us. On top of that, we face deciding whether or not hormone replacement therapy is the right option to deal with these changes.

How can women view the phase of life called menopause realistically, and approach it and live through it without fear? Knowledge and preparation are the keys that open the door, inviting us all to enter our middle and later years of life more in control than ever of our bodies, our emotions, and our lives.

Many women experience a new calmness after their bodies release the intensity of their monthly hormone cycles. These women suggest that the menopausal transition is a time to listen to your body, hear what it is telling you, accept the changes it is making, and embrace the new person you are becoming.

After our bodies complete menopause, we are free to enjoy sexual intercourse without fear of pregnancy. But then our pelvic organs begin to change because they are no longer stimulated by estrogen. At the same time, our appearance begins to change, and we fear no longer feeling attractive and desirable because we have heard that our youthful feminine appearance is largely controlled by our hormones.

HRT seems to provide the instant answer, a woman's fountain of youth, by boosting the hormone levels in our bodies and stopping the aging clock. But it isn't that simple. Although HRT can benefit a woman's appearance in some ways, it does not stop the natural aging process, and it can have side effects. The seriousness of the side effects depends on a woman's own individual health profile.

Today, experts believe the risks of developing breast or uterine cancer, heart disease, and osteoporosis can be traced through your family health history. Your health risks can also be affected by your age, diet, lifestyle, and the kind of replacement hormones you take.

A large percentage of women in America pass through menopause into later life with ease, in comfort, and able to maintain their good health. Women in other cultures breeze through menopause with no adverse effects. We can learn a lot from these women and integrate their secrets into our own lives. By regulating the hormone balance within our bodies, our good health and radiant appearance can be maintained and enhanced. As a result, our self-confidence and sense of stability will enable us to maintain inner peace. Then we can handle whatever discomfort and distress menopause may bring to us because we'll feel good enough physically and emotionally to continue living the full, useful lives we have created for ourselves.

How can you regulate the hormone balance within your body to offset the discomforts of menopause as your ovaries gradually produce fewer hormones? Conventional medicine often prescribes HRT and suggests accompanying dietary and lifestyle changes. That approach is effective, and safe, for many women. Other women prefer more natural hormones, programs, and remedies that may include nutritional supplements, herbs, or acupuncture, with the guidance of alternative health care professionals, along with dietary and lifestyle changes. Many women combine elements of these various approaches. Every woman is unique.

How do you decide what is right for you? First, learn as much as you can about your own body and about the health care options available to you. Talk with health care professionals you trust, those who really listen to you and seem genuinely interested in your well-being. Talk with other women about their experiences and yours. Read about menopause and women's health care. Write down what you know, learn, and feel about menopause. Do not limit yourself to a single point of view or program based on the advice of anyone, whether it's from a health care professional or a friend. This decision is yours alone to make.

What if you try something and it doesn't seem to be working right away? After making educated and informed health care choices based on what feels right to you and embarking on a health care program, give it a reasonable period of time before deciding whether it's effective. Even though you have a right to change your mind as often as you choose, your body may need time to catch up with your mind. The hormonal system of your body is complicated; constant, sudden changes will only confuse it. This is a time to be gentle with your body—and with yourself.

Now, more than ever, the mature woman recognizes that the ultimate responsibility for her own emotional and physical well-being is hers alone. Women have become seekers. We gather information, we weigh what we have learned, and finally, we seek to apply that knowledge to our own lives.

This book does not take a position. It does not presume to tell you what is best for you. It presents the facts about hormone replacement therapy that you need to consider before choosing from your health care options.

Question 1

What's Really Happening to My Body During Menopause?

If you are in the age range of forty-eight to fifty-two you've probably already started to experience changes in your body that are undeniably signs of menopause. Although you may not want to talk about it, or even think about it, eventually your body will demand that you pay attention to the significant changes that are occurring in how it functions.

The natural transition a woman's body makes from the reproductive phase of life into the nonreproduction stage actually begins during her thirties, when production of hormones by the ovaries starts to diminish gradually. As early as the mid-thirties and into the mid-forties, hormone production may become erratic. Although some women are not aware of these changes, others experience premenopause, a preview of menopause, with sometimes irregular menstrual periods, irritability, mood swings, changes in memory retention, aches and pains, unexpected body temperature fluctuations, loss of energy, and sleep disturbances.[1]

1. Menstrual irregularity, hot flashes, and night sweats before premenopausal or menopausal age may be symptoms of a serious health condition; therefore, immediately tell your physician if you experience any of these symptoms.

While every woman's menopausal transitional experience is different, one thing is certain: Eventually your ovaries will stop producing enough hormones to support the reproductive cycle, and your menstrual periods will stop altogether.[2]

When your menstrual periods become consistently irregular or stop altogether during your mid- to late forties or mid-fifties (late menopause), it's most likely menopause that you're "going through." If you didn't feel the effects of your diminishing hormones during the premenopausal years, now you may begin to experience the discomforts associated with menopause. Every woman's experiences are unique. Some women experience no menopausal discomfort at all—their menstrual periods just stop one day; others experience the entire array of discomforts while their periods are still regular.

Do I Need Medical Treatment for Menopause?

At least 50 percent of women do nothing about menopause because they consider it a normal transition in life.

Women most likely to seek medical assistance during menopause are those experiencing severe menopausal discomfort or those at risk for developing serious health conditions that can occur during the middle and later years of life when hormone production changes. After a woman's body has made the hormonal adjustments, she faces postmenopausal changes in her body that may require serious attention in order for her to maintain optimal health into her later years of life.

Many women consult a physician when their menstrual periods become irregular in order to find out what's happening in their bod-

2. When a woman's ovaries are surgically removed before she reaches natural menopause, she will go through menopause immediately.

ies; or, after their periods initially stop they wonder if they might be pregnant. (It is possible to become pregnant after your periods have stopped, so doctors advise that you should wait one year before discontinuing birth control.) Although a simple blood test can determine whether your body has menopausal hormone levels, blood hormone levels in many women become so erratic during the menopausal transition that menopause could be indicated by the test one week and the next week the results could be different.

Be sure to report to your doctor all discomforts or symptoms of abnormal health conditions you are experiencing, especially heart palpitations or bone discomfort. Now is the time to be very candid with your doctor about your personal health history and any medications you take—prescription and over-the-counter—and to discuss your genetic family health history in detail. This information provides a road map you and your doctor can follow to determine what your future health care needs may be, what preventive health care you may need, and what lifestyle changes may be beneficial. Various medical evaluations may be required to ensure that you are not at risk for serious immediate or long-term health conditions.

As your menopause proceeds, your doctor may want to schedule regular checkup appointments. The frequency of those visits usually depends on your current health status, your health risks, and any medications you are taking, including HRT if you decide it is the right choice for you.

The average period of time during which a woman is aware of her menopausal transition is usually five to seven years, although some women may not know for sure when it starts or when it's over.

After your body has made the hormonal adjustment, completing menopause, postmenopausal changes that occur in your body may require serious attention or lifestyle changes in order for you to maintain optimal health into the later years of life. The likelihood that you'll have postmenopausal health problems that could lead to serious disorders or disease is based on your personal health status, genetic family health history, lifestyle, and dietary habits before menopause, during menopause, after menopause, and into later life.

How Much Do I Need to Know About How My Body Functions?

Woman who approach the menopausal years understanding how the female body functions and what changes can be anticipated are better prepared to navigate the menopausal transition, as well as make decisions about their health care choices without fear and confusion.

The major changes in how the female body operates after menopause occur mainly because the ovaries stop producing the hormones estrogen and progesterone, which are necessary for reproduction. When estrogen is produced in the ovaries by ripening egg follicles, it stimulates the uterus, causing the uterine lining to build up during reproductive years. After a mature egg is released by the ovaries (ovulation), progesterone production begins. Progesterone prepares the uterine lining to be implanted with a fertilized egg, resulting in pregnancy. If a fertilized egg does not implant in the uterus, progesterone levels drop off dramatically, triggering the uterus to shed the endometrial lining (menstrual period).

Progesterone, which is also produced by the ovaries, is an intermediate building block for other hormones within the female body. When your body produces abnormal levels of progesterone, your menstrual cycles will become irregular.

Studies indicate most women stop producing progesterone first. Estrogen production by the ovaries and uterus continues in varying degrees until some time after the completion of menopause. Irregular menstrual cycles, which are common in otherwise healthy menopausal-age women, usually indicate diminishing levels of hormones or erratic production of hormones by the ovaries. Ovulation stops when the ovaries have run out of eggs to ripen or when the eggs are too old. That's when your menstrual periods stop, too.

What Do Estrogen and Progestrone Do in Your Body?

Every part of your body is affected by estrogen, which is a cellular stimulant. Three types of estrogen are produced by your body: the ovaries produce estradiol, the strongest estrogen, which contributes to monthly ovulation and normal menstrual cycles; a less potent estrogen, estrone, is converted from elements of fatty tissue; and an even weaker estrogen, estriol, results from estradiol and estrone metabolism within the body.

When ovarian production of estrogen diminishes, the adrenal glands take over, producing estrone, a weaker form of estrogen. Although the estrogen produced by the adrenal glands is a much less potent form of estrogen than that produced by the ovaries, it can help to alleviate some common discomforts associated with menopause, such as hot flashes, excessive sweating, inability to sleep, and vaginal dryness. A woman with healthy adrenal glands usually experiences an easier menopause with less physical discomfort.

The body also continues to convert androgens (male hormones) from body fat into estrone during and after menopause. Heavier women usually have higher estrogen levels than thin women during menopause and may experience a smoother transition. However, it is well known that too much body fat is detrimental to the overall health of a woman in many ways. Entering menopause at an appropriate weight for your body type and maintaining that weight through adequate nutritional intake and exercise is best for your overall good health.

Very thin women often experience menopause earlier in life.

When Can I Expect the Menopausal Transition to Begin?

Menopause usually begins between the ages of forty-eight and fifty-two. Obvious hormonal changes such as irritability, mood swings, sleep disturbances, changes in memory retention, and aches and pains can begin as early as thirty-five or forty—five to ten years before the actual onset of menopause. This is especially true for women who suffer from PMS, ovarian cysts, endometriosis, fibroid tumors, or other disorders associated with female hormone imbalances.

An early menopause may occur during a woman's early forties. Premature menopause (loss of ovarian hormone production before the age of forty) has been known to occur in women as young as twenty, but that is rare. Still, a woman with intact ovaries may experience premature menopause if she has fewer eggs than normal, causing her ovaries to stop producing estrogen earlier than the average. Premature menopause may also result if a woman has surgery that cuts off the blood supply to the ovaries, or receives chemotherapy or radiation treatments for cancer, or if severe infections have damaged the ovaries or destroyed ovarian tissue.

Many factors influence the age at which your menopause begins, as well as your degree of discomfort and the eventual development of menopause-related health problems. Among these factors are heredity; hormone production; your overall health and lifestyle, including diet, exercise, stress, alcohol intake, smoking, and toxin exposure; and even the altitude at which you live.

You may notice when looking at your biological family the similar genetic material revealed by body types, skin color, hair color, and more. Your genetic makeup also indicates a pattern of hormonal function within your body, which may translate to menopausal pattern similarities among your female biological forebears, female siblings, and yourself. Because the quality of life has changed dramatically during the past century, with life expectancy increasing, a woman today may not go through menopause at exactly the same age as her mother and grandmothers, but a genetic predisposition toward early or late menopause may show up.

Am I Doing Anything That Would Cause an Early Menopause?

Your lifestyle can definitely influence when your body will begin manifesting symptoms of menopause, how easy or difficult your menopausal transition might be, and your postmenopausal health. Beginning with your overall health, factors such as diet, stress, physical activity, smoking, drinking, and environmental toxin exposure can also affect when your menopause begins and how smoothly you make the transition. Here's a brief rundown:

- Your overall health, which is definitely influenced by your lifestyle, can determine how well your body adjusts to the changes it's undergoing during menopause and afterward. The ovaries are glands that interact with various other glands located throughout your body, creating the endocrine system. Secretions from the glands stimulate and support every part of your body. When one of these glands stops producing hormones, it affects all the rest. The body then attempts to rebalance itself naturally. If your body does not need to expend energy overcoming existing health problems, then it can adjust more easily to the changes of menopause.

- Negative stress can be detrimental to the body at any time, but unmanaged stress can increase hormone imbalances leading up to and during menopause, magnifying emotional and physical discomforts you may already be feeling. Ongoing unmanaged stress sends your body into an extended fight-or-flight mode, causing the adrenal glands to continually kick in, providing extra survival energy. Adrenal exhaustion can result, leaving your body unequipped to handle emotional and physical exertion of any kind. Moreover, the adrenal glands are then unavailable to convert androgens into estrogen when the ovaries are unable to do so. Since the adrenal glands play specific roles within the complicated endocrine system, loss of adrenal function at a time when you most need it affects your entire body. This can have a destructive effect on your menopausal transition, as well as your future health, especially your skeletal and cardiovascular systems. Chapter 7 offers many suggestions for how you can reduce the impact of negative stress on your health.
- Women who regularly consume substantial amounts of alcoholic beverages go through menopause earlier than those who do not. Excessive alcohol consumption is detrimental to any woman's overall health.
- Studies suggest that smoking cigarettes affects a woman's estrogen levels, in addition to the other damage it inflicts on

the body. Reports also indicate that smokers go through menopause one to two years earlier than nonsmokers or ex-smokers. The longer a woman has smoked and the number of cigarettes she smoked daily seems to move her closer to an early menopause. Women who live with smokers and are exposed to passive cigarette smoke also seem to enter menopause earlier, as do women whose mothers smoked.

Smokers are also at higher risk for developing health problems during their postmenopausal years, including osteoporosis and cardiovascular diseases and disorders.

- We are only beginning to understand how exposure to toxic substances affects a woman's health, but the news is not good. Contact with chemicals in soil and water is being linked to higher risks of developing breast cancer, endometriosis, and osteoporosis, as well as being generally detrimental to a woman's overall health. Avoiding pesticides and chemicals, including those contained in household cleaning products, is better for your body and for the environment.
- Although the reasons are not clear, studies have shown that women who live at higher altitudes enter menopause years earlier than women who live at lower altitudes.

What Can I Expect Might Happen to My Body During Menopause?

As your body attempts to adjust to diminishing or erratic production of hormones by the ovaries, the following signs of menopause may cause physical and emotional discomfort or distress but usually not serious health conditions:

- Irregular menstrual periods are common. Your menstrual periods will probably change. Sometimes menstrual cycles become shorter and diminish, sometimes they become longer with increased flow. Some women's periods just stop one day and never resume. Your menstrual periods may also begin to be accompanied by cramping and clotted blood flow.
- Hot flashes may occur initially at night, and then during the day, especially after eating or physical activity. They seem to occur most often before the onset of a menstrual period and are sometimes stronger when the period is delayed. It's common for sweating to occur during the flush of a hot flash. Leg cramping may occur at night. If you have heart palpitations along with hot flashes, as some women do, please report this to your physician, as they may be a symptom of a serious health condition.
- Sleep disturbances may result because of hot flashes, night sweating, and leg cramping.
- Emotional changes or sudden changes of temperament may include fatigue, depression, anxiety, mood swings, irritability, aggression, insomnia, and even compulsive eating.
- Disorders of the reproductive organs, such as uterine fibroids and ovarian cysts, may be discovered during a physical examination or medical tests.
- Vaginal secretions will probably increase or decrease.

What Changes Can I Expect in My Body After Menopause?

Diminished ovarian hormone production causes the cells, tissues, and organs within the body that were supported and stimulated by those hormones to change. The parts of your body most affected are those that functioned within the reproductive process. Although these changes occur gradually in every woman's body, your experiences will not be exactly like anyone else's. They manifest differently, to a greater or lesser degree, and within different periods of time, some immediately, many very much later in life.

After your periods have stopped because menopause has concluded, eventually you will notice changes in your pelvic organs, your appearance, your breasts, your bones, and your cardiovascular system. All of these changes can be affected by your lifestyle and whether you decide to take HRT. Some changes will be noticed sooner than others, and some require serious consideration of your long-term health care needs.

The changes you are likely to notice sooner are:

- Vaginal changes, including vaginal dryness, which can lead to a loss of sexual interest; vaginal shrinkage and appearance changes in the vaginal area.
- Mucous membranes of the vagina and vulva become more fragile and are more easily damaged, possibly causing you to bleed during or after intercourse.
- Urinary tract changes that may lead to increased frequency of urination and urgency to urinate, or to urinary tract infections.
- Vaginal and bladder infections sometimes occur more frequently.
- Lower abdominal congestion, which can cause bloating, difficult digestion, constipation, and hemorrhoids. These conditions may be accompanied by headaches.
- Changes in your appearance, which are part of the natural aging process, including body shape changes and redistribution of fat.

Pelvic Organs: Vaginal Changes

The vagina and surrounding tissues are among the most sensitive estrogen-dependent parts of your body. Besides vaginal dryness, which can result in painful intercourse and lead to a loss of sexual interest, appearance and structural changes take place in and around the vagina after menopause when estrogen production within the body diminishes dramatically. Thinning of pubic hair and wrinkling of the vulva as skin loses elasticity and some fat content result from hormonal changes, as well as the natural aging process. The labia may become less sensitive and be less likely to swell and separate during sexual stimulation.

Eventually your vagina will begin to atrophy. Before menopause, the estrogen-rich vaginal lining is normally several layers thick. Lack of estrogen during menopause causes the vaginal tissue to become thinner and more fragile, losing elasticity and lubricating capability, and causing it to change shape. Before menopause, the vagina is normally two-and-a-half to four inches long, with the cervix protruding into the vagina. After menopause, the vagina tends to constrict, becoming shorter and narrower close to the cervix, which tends to flatten. The vagina does not stretch as easily and is more prone to damage and bleeding when penetrated, which can result in uncomfortable sexual intercourse.

After menopause, when the estrogen-deficient vaginal lining is reduced to only a few layers of cells, the vagina is more prone to infection or inflammation. It can cause vaginitis, a burning and itching feeling, sometimes accompanied by an unpleasant yellow or light green vaginal discharge, bleeding, or spotting.

Vaginal bleeding is most commonly caused by vaginal atrophy, but it can also be a warning sign that something more serious is happening in your body. If vaginal bleeding occurs after your menstrual periods have stopped it should be discussed with your physician so the cause can be determined, especially if you are taking HRT.

Vaginal bleeding can be confused with bleeding from the urinary bladder or urethra. Postmenopausal bleeding can be a warning sign that there are abnormalities of the uterine lining.

Most women have vaginal atrophy to some degree after menopause. The extent to which a woman's pelvic organs change after menopause depends on her individual genetic profile and her overall health and lifestyle. Every woman is different, but vaginal atrophy usually develops three to ten years after menopause, with the average being four to five years after a woman's last menstrual period. Vaginal dryness and painful intercourse are usually the first signs of vaginal atrophy. Frequent vaginal bleeding after intercourse, persistent vaginal irritation, or infections need to be reported to your physician.

How Can My Doctor Tell If My Vagina Is Atrophying?

The premenopausal, estrogen-rich vaginal lining is pink, thick, and well lubricated, with many folds. After vaginal atrophy has developed it will look thin, dry, and flattened. The estrogen levels in your vagina can be measured by a maturation index (also called an estrogen index), which is performed by your doctor scraping cells from the vaginal wall in the same way a Pap smear is taken from the cervix.

Pelvic Organs: Uterine Changes

Women who experienced problems involving the uterus before menopause, such as fibroid tumors and endometriosis, will be pleased to know that once hormone stimulation ceases, those problems are likely to diminish, or even disappear completely.

At one time it was common for doctors to suggest that women have hysterectomies to remove the uterus after menopause. This was particularly true when women were taking unopposed estrogen after menopause, which has a detrimental effect on the uterus. Since we now know that progestins are also needed when a woman takes supplemental estrogen after menopause, women are less likely to agree to unnecessary hysterectomies, which present an entirely different set of problems afterward.

In time the uterus will change shape and may shift a bit in location, dropping down and applying pressure on the bladder and urinary tract.

Pelvic Organs: Bladder and Urinary Tract Changes

Urinary tract changes in your body may lead not only to increased frequency of urination and the urgency to urinate, but also to urinary tract infections.

A woman's urinary bladder, located in the front of the pelvic cavity, sits on top of her vagina and cervix. Her urethra, the one-and-one-half-inch tube that carries urine from the bladder out of the body, runs along the top portion of the vaginal wall, emptying just above the vaginal opening. The urethra and bladder are supported by the same estrogen-sensitive tissues as the vagina. Loss of estrogen can cause the tissues of the urinary tract and bladder to become thinner and to atrophy, making them more vulnerable to infection by organisms they were once able to resist. Recurrent bladder infections and urinary incontinence may result. In severe cases, a woman's bladder and uterus may drop, causing numerous physical problems.

A woman may suspect bladder or urethra atrophy if she feels a burning sensation while urinating, if she develops a need to urinate more frequently, if she feels an urgent need to urinate, if she has difficulty holding her urine, or if she involuntarily wets her pants. These symptoms can occur because of bladder inflammations or infections, usually accompanied by some pain, but they may also occur without infection.

Urinary incontinence can occur before menopause as well as after. Premenopausal urinary incontinence usually is not related to lack of estrogen. Some women have an inherited tendency for weak connective tissue between the vagina and its supportive structures. More often, premenopausal urinary incontinence results from the vagina and its supportive tissues being weakened during childbirth, especially in women who have had more than one large baby or who had significant vaginal tearing.

Urinary incontinence that first occurs after menopause is usually related to loss of estrogen. Often it is a progressive condition that begins with stress incontinence. Stress incontinence is the uncontrollable loss of urine that occurs when a woman sneezes, coughs, laughs, jumps rope, or exercises.

Menopausal or postmenopausal stress incontinence is usually related to estrogen loss, when the muscle tissues surrounding the urethra become weakened and less elastic. Then, the urethral lining may be unable to control the release of urine, or the angle between the urethra and the bladder may change so urine is not prevented from dripping under sudden pressure.

Stress incontinence may also be related to emotional stress. If stress incontinence occurs suddenly after an extreme emotional upset, the condition may subside in time and with emotional healing.

While taking estrogen can contribute to a woman's maintaining her bladder control well into the later years, eventually the natural aging process will result in some loss of nerve supply to the bladder.

A natural means of strengthening and toning the muscles around the bladder and rectum to improve mild stress incontinence is the Kegel exercises. To perform the Kegel exercises, tighten the muscles around the vagina, bladder, and rectum by squeezing your vagina and buttocks, then releasing them. Repeat this exercise twenty to thirty times several times a day. You can do them anytime and anywhere. Also, when you urinate, stop the flow, hold it for a few seconds, then allow it to continue.

After doing the Kegel exercises for several months, most women feel a marked improvement in the tone of their pelvic muscles. The exercises also tone the vaginal muscles and tighten the entrance to the vagina.

Changes in Your Appearance

Changes in your appearance will gradually become obvious to you, including body shape changes, skin that is drier and begins to wrinkle, and fingernails that break more easily.

Body shape changes and redistribution of fat during menopause are not uncommon, with many women experiencing some fat accumulation in the stomach area and thighs. Although this may seem upsetting as it occurs, it may also be beneficial by plumping up skin that is naturally losing its firmness, especially after menopause. A little extra fat may also help alleviate the discomforts of menopause because the body converts the androgens in fat to estrogen.

Appearance Changes: Your Weight

It is generally agreed that menopause does not cause weight gain, although some weight gain is a natural part of the aging process. Excessive weight gain and fluid retention associated with the menopausal years is usually related to lack of exercise and poor eating habits. Women taking HRT have reported weight gain associated with it.

Weight gain or weight loss can also be associated with thyroid gland malfunction. The thyroid gland, located in the lower throat area, regulates a woman's metabolism. When thyroid function is too low (hypothyroidism), a woman may experience weight gain, lack of energy, dry skin, brittle nails, dull hair (sometimes accompanied by hair thinning), a slow pulse, and intolerance to cold. When thyroid function is too high (hyperthroidism), a woman may experience weight loss, feelings of anxiety and nervousness, inability to relax even when tired, a fast pulse, intolerance to heat, and sometimes heart palpitations.

Thyroid gland malfunction is also believed to cause estrogen imbalances in the body.

What causes the thyroid gland to malfunction? The reasons any gland malfunctions in the endocrine system are not easily determined because the function of one gland affects the others. The ovaries are one of the seven primary endocrine glands; the others are the pancreas, adrenals, thymus, thyroid, pituitary, and hypothalamus. Thyroid imbalances seem to occur during premenopause because the thyroid gland interacts with the pituitary gland as it attempts to stimulate ovulation. Stress has a dramatic effect on thyroid function one way or the other. Diet and nutritional intake may also affect your thyroid gland function.

Your physician can conduct various blood tests to evaluate your thyroid function. Keep in mind that various medications can affect thyroid tests, so be sure to tell your doctor if you are taking HRT or birth control pills, aspirin, cough medicine containing iodine, corticosteroids, or Dilantin.

Appearance Changes: Your Skin

Skin, the largest organ of the body, seems to be especially sensitive to the hormonal changes taking place in a woman's body during menopause. The skin has a thin outer layer called the epidermis, and a thick, deeper layer called the *dermis*. The dermis, composed mostly of protein collagen and elastin fibers, also contains blood vessels, sensory nerves, and lymph, oil, and sweat glands that nourish hair follicles and the thin epidermal layer. Collagen makes your skin thick, toned, and elastic.

The cells of the skin are constantly renewing themselves in the same way all the other cells in your body are, with the assistance of hormones that break down the old cells and stimulate the growth of healthy new ones.

As a woman's hormone production decreases, so does the ability of her skin cells to reproduce, resulting in less collagen. In turn the skin becomes thinner, with less fat and muscle to support it, as well as having diminished moisture content. At the same time the deep tissues are contracting, the thin upper layer of skin becomes less elastic and resilient. Eventually, as the natural aging process occurs, skin starts to sag and wrinkle.

Appearance Changes: Your Hair

Estrogen stimulates the growth of sexual hair on a woman's body and inhibits the growth of unwanted hair on the face, legs, and arms. During menopause, as estrogen production diminishes, it is not uncommon for a woman to see a decrease in her pubic hair and underarm hair. Sometimes the hair on a woman's head becomes drier and coarser during menopause.

While estrogen production becomes erratic or diminishes, the body continues to produce androgens, causing an imbalance that may result in growth of unwanted hair on the legs, and arms, and sometimes a few coarse hairs on a woman's chin or the side of her face.

Depending on your genetic makeup, the hair on your head may gradually thin. The follicles that contain the roots of hairs are located in the deep tissue layer of the skin. During menopause, when estrogen levels drop or become erratic, the tissue surrounding the hair follicles loses collagen and provides less support. Blood flow and energy flow through the nerves, also located in the deep skin layer, may decrease as well, providing less nourishment to the hair follicles.

Stress can cause hair thinning and hair loss by depleting the body of essential B vitamins and causing blood flow to the skin and hair follicles to be diminished.

Long-Term Body Changes

What Long-term Changes in My Body Can I Expect?

Although long-term changes in your body usually occur gradually, by the time you reach menopause they have already started taking place and require that you seriously consider your long-term health care options as soon as possible. The decisions you make now should be based on your current health condition, your health risks, whether HRT can be beneficial for you (as discussed in Chapters 3 through 5), your current lifestyle, and how committed you are to making necessary lifestyle changes.

The long-term changes that have already started in your body, but may not be obvious to you until a health crisis brings them to your attention, are as follows:

- Bone changes, depending on the condition of a woman's bones, connective tissue, and her capacity to retain and absorb calcium, could include aches and pains in joints, fallen arches of the feet, or pinched disks between the spinal vertebrae. Extreme bone changes can lead to osteoporosis.
- As breasts change, they begin to lose their buoyancy and start to droop. Some women's breasts become sore or develop hypersensitive masses. Because the onset of breast disease is common after menopause, mammograms are recommended by the American Cancer Society.
- Circulatory changes may be evident in varicose veins or feelings of heaviness and cramping in the legs. Extreme circulatory changes could lead to high blood pressure, heart disease, or stroke.

Long-term Body Changes: Your Bones

Bone is living tissue (made of calcium phosphate crystals connected by collagen protein fibers) that needs constant nourishment and stimulation to remain healthy and strong. Hormones stimulate the bones, helping them to absorb nutrients, break down aging bone tissue, and to build healthy new bone, a process called *bone remodeling*. Estrogen stimulates osteoclasts, the cells that break down aging bone cells, dissolve them, and clear a space for new bone to be created. Progesterone stimulates osteoblasts.The cells that then come along and form new bone. The process of bone remodeling keeps bones strong and flexible and prevents them from getting dry and brittle.

Adequate levels of hormones are necessary for the body to continue this process of breaking down aging bone cells and rebuilding new healthy bone. Without hormones, your body cannot properly use calcium, minerals, vitamins, and other nutrients for bone remodeling, and osteoporosis can develop.

Bones have various functions in the body. They create the framework for the body, they protect our organs, they support our muscles, and they are the warehouse where our body stores minerals. Minerals are essential for the proper function of every part of our bodies, but our bodies can't make minerals; we must get them from our food and supplements. Blood and fluids circulate through our bones, just as they do through the rest of our body. The fluids supply nutrients to the bones, and at the same time they draw minerals from our bones and carry them to other parts of our bodies where they are needed. Our bones stay strong when they can constantly renew their supply of nutrients from the blood and fluid circulating within them.

Osteoporosis

Osteoporosis is an excessive deterioration of the bones that leaves them thin and brittle. It develops when the calcium crystals and protein fibers do not get enough nourishment to rebuild and renew themselves to stay strong and flexible. This can happen because we are not taking in and assimilating enough nutrients or because the bone's nutrient warehouse is being emptied to supply other parts of our bodies. As our bodies age, they need more calcium and minerals.

The effects of osteoporosis usually show up in the later years of life, when bones have deteriorated so much that they easily fracture and break, often causing disability. But because osteoporosis is progressive, it can be avoided or arrested by understanding how the body ages and by taking appropriate action.

Osteoporosis does not appear to be caused by one particular thing but by a combination of factors. Worldwide studies have been useful in defining the risk factors of developing osteoporosis as they are currently understood, based on age, hormone production, heredity, body type, and lifestyle.

If you are healthy, your bones develop and grow stronger until you reach your thirties. At that point, as your hormone production begins to drop, your bones slowly begin to lose mineral content until menopause begins.

After menopause, when your ovaries stop producing hormones, or when your ovaries are surgically removed, comes the period of greatest bone loss, which lasts for three to ten years, depending on your individual health. Then the rate of bone loss slows down but continues for the rest of your life.

Does Every Woman Eventually Develop Osteoporosis?

Statistics say that as high as 50 percent of American women are calcium deficient, which can lead to osteoporosis. Approximately 35 percent of all women show some evidence of osteoporosis by age sixty and 25 percent experience a hip fracture by age eighty.

Heredity and your body type and ethnicity are predictors of your risk of developing osteoporosis. You may need to be more concerned about your bone health if you fit into these higher-risk categories:

- Caucasian or Asian female with fair or translucent skin
- A history of osteoporosis or hip fracture in your biological family
- A slender body or one with low muscle mass

Experts believe that osteoporosis probably is hereditary, and there are ongoing studies to isolate the gene that causes it. The genetic predisposition to developing osteoporosis may also be related to inherited hormonal patterns in a woman.

Thin women usually enter menopause earlier than heavier women, and heavier women have higher levels of estrogen during and after menopause. Heavier women stress their bones more in everyday movement because there is more weight pressure on their bones. Also, during and after menopause, as lower levels of hormones are being produced by your ovaries, hormones can be converted from body fat to offset glandular hormonal production decreases. Perhaps that's why many women develop body fat in the stomach area around the time of menopause. This may be the body's way of creating a natural storehouse of hormones to be used when needed.

Still, being overweight is never beneficial for your overall health. Maintaining an appropriate, healthy weight for your body type is the best way to stay healthy at any time of life.

Conclusion

Menopause is a natural physical transition from one stage of life to another and does not necessarily cause serious health problems, although health problems are more likely to develop during the middle and later years of life. Because menopause has a dramatic effect within your body, your health status before and during menopause is usually an indicator of your health afterward. Of course, health-affirming lifestyle choices are most beneficial for your long-term physical and emotional well-being.

Question 2

What Can I Do to Alleviate My Menopausal Symptoms?

Every woman's menopausal "transitional experience" is different. Some women are so dramatically affected by the physical symptoms commonly associated with menopause that they feel as though they are living in someone else's body. Other women experience no change in their bodies at all, except that eventually their menstrual periods stop. You may feel mild physical or emotional symptoms.

The most common complaints of women during menopause include hot flashes, often accompanied by heart palpitations and night sweats that cause sleep disturbances; lack of energy; vaginal dryness; loss of sexual desire; and body aches and pains. Other changes may include mood swings, anxiety, nervousness, or feelings of instability; reduced memory retention; inability to concentrate; depression; and sleep disturbances unrelated to night sweats.

A combination estrogen/progestin type of HRT often alleviates the discomforts most women experience during menopause. Women in extreme distress, both physically and emotionally, during their menopausal transition have said that HRT helped them regain control of their lives. However, a period of experimentation may be needed in order to find just the right dosage that works for each individual. Women have reported that one of the main reasons they stopped taking HRT soon after they started it was because of side effects and difficulty in finding the right dosage. Other women prefer the milder, more natural estrogen/natural progesterone combination preparations.

The severity of menopausal discomfort or distress may be a determining factor in your decision about taking HRT or continuing to do so. It is extremely important for every woman choosing to take HRT of any type to realistically assess the health risks specific to her individual health status and family health history. These risk factors must be completely disclosed and honestly discussed with your physician.

Many women forego taking HRT altogether, opting instead for lifestyle changes and seeking the advice of alternative health care providers such as acupuncturists, chiropractors, herbalists, or nutritionists. There are many simple techniques and nondrug therapies women can use to reduce the discomforts of menopause. These can be particularly helpful for a woman who cannot take HRT or chooses not to take it, or when used in conjunction with HRT to lower her dosage requirements.

Understanding what is happening in your body can help you make a decision about whether HRT is right for you.

Hot Flashes

A hot flash is a sudden rush of hot energy, usually starting around the breasts and spreading upward to the neck, face, and head. It may be accompanied by sweating, heart palpitations, and a cold, damp feeling on the skin.

One supportive husband was overheard saying to his wife, "It's not a hot flash, it's a power surge."

Not all women have hot flashes. At least 10 percent of menopausal women never have a hot flash; 80 percent have them from time to time, but do not find them disturbing; and 10 percent report having severe hot flashes, which are extremely uncomfortable.

What Causes Hot Flashes

Hot flashes are related to the erratic production of hormones by the ovaries. Although no one knows for sure what causes hot flashes, it is believed they are a result of complex interactions between the ovaries and the brain. This process probably involves the pituitary gland as it attempts to stimulate the ovaries into producing hormones, the hypothalamus (the part of the brain that controls body temperature), and the adrenal glands as they attempt to kick in and take over production of estrogen when the ovaries begin to stop producing it.

The body becomes hotter inside and blood flow to the skin increases in an effort to cool it down. As a result, the skin temperature rises and the heart rate increases. The skin may become red and sweating may occur. As the perspiration evaporates the skin becomes cold, pale, and damp feeling. In a small percentage of women, the effects are severe, can feel debilitating, and may be embarrassing. If you experience severe hot flashes, especially if you have heart palpitations along with them, please be sure to tell your physician. Precautionary medical tests may be indicated in order to determine whether a serious health problem exists or is developing, apart from menopause.

Some women report that other discomforts, such as dizziness or headaches, accompany their hot flashes. Other women report that hot flashes are extremely uncomfortable, with accompanying profuse sweating and frightening heart palpitations; however, these are rare. Most women are hardly bothered by hot flashes, even when they are aware that they are happening.

How Long Do Hot Flashes Last?

A hot flash usually subsides within five minutes; however, every woman's experiences are different, with some reporting hot flashes that lasted as long as half an hour. Usually a woman senses a hot flash before it happens. This preflush period lasts for one to four minutes before the hot flash actually begins, then the sudden hot feeling occurs and a wave of heat spreads upward from the chest through the body.

Among women who do experience hot flashes, most say they occur for one or two years, but about 30 percent have them for five years or longer. Because hot flashes are related to erratic hormone production by the ovaries, which can last for several years, the patterns of frequency and duration of hot flashes often change. You may have them for a short period of time and never have them again, they may occur on and off for longer periods of time, or they may stop for a while and then recur.

Are Hot Flashes Triggered by Something?

Many women want to know when hot flashes usually occur. Although unpredictable, they often occur during the night. When they do occur during the day, it can be as a result of the following circumstances:

- A sudden fright caused by a loud noise or unexpected sound
- Situations that are emotionally stressful
- Drinking hot liquids or eating hot or spicy foods
- Consumption of alcoholic beverages

Although hot flashes can be embarrassing when they are severe and occur in public, this rarely happens. Probably the most disturbing aspect of hot flashes is that they frequently occur at night and wake a woman from her sleep. The sweating can also make sleepwear and bedding wet. Nighttime hot flashes can have a dramatic impact on a woman during menopause by interrupting her sleep enough to lead to tiredness and lack of energy. This can also contribute to emotional problems associated with sleep deprivation, such as irritability, anxiety, disorientation, nervousness, and even depression.

Can Hot Flashes Be Prevented?

HRT is often effective for preventing hot flashes. In addition to HRT, or instead of it, nutritional and alternative medical therapies can also help alleviate hot flashes. They include dietary changes, nutritional supplements, herbs, homeopathic remedies, and Ayurveda.

Dietary changes definitely assist the body's ability to adjust to temperature variations. Besides the overall health-enhancing diet discussed in Chapter 7, hot flashes can be alleviated by avoiding large meals, spicy foods, and coffee, and by eating a diet rich in phytoestrogens, foods that have an estrogenic effect in the body. In fact, the infrequency of hot flashes experienced by Asian women is associated with their high intake of soy-based foods, which are phytoestrogens. Other foods that may help hot flashes are alfalfa, almonds, apples, carrots, cashew nuts, corn, cucumbers, oats, peanuts, peas, pomegranate seeds, wheat, and yams.

It is also important to drink plenty of fresh, clean water to help regulate your body temperature, especially during warm weather or when your body is overheated from exercise.

Nutritional supplements that have been shown to help alleviate hot flashes include the following:

- Vitamin E at 400 IU twice daily helps regulate estrogen in the body. Add the trace mineral selenium at 100 mcg daily to enhance heart function and help regulate body temperature.
- Vitamin C at 500 to 1,000 mg with each meal supports adrenal gland function, enhances the effectiveness of estrogen, helps regulate body temperature, and strengthens capillaries. A vitamin C supplement with bioflavonoids is even better. It tones blood vessel walls and reduces their dilation during a hot flash.
- B complex, containing at least 50 mg of each primary B vitamin, twice daily, enhances the effectiveness of estrogen in the body.
- Additional vitamin B_5 (pantothenic acid), at 200 to 500 mg daily, supports adrenal gland function.
- Additional PABA (a member of the B-vitamin complex) helps keep estrogen levels higher for longer periods of time.
- Bee pollen contains both male and female hormones and can help relieve hot flashes as well as other discomforts of menopause. Take around 500 mg a day, but discontinue if you develop allergic reaction symptoms similar to hay fever.

Herbs that have been shown to alleviate hot flashes include ginseng, damiana, dong quai, passion flower, and sarsaparilla. Your health care professional might also suggest you take other herbs to help ease your body through the menopausal transition.

Homeopathic remedies that can relieve hot flashes are *Belladonna*, *Ferrum metallicum*, *Lachesis*, *Pulsatilla*, *Sanguinaria*, and *Valeriana*. Your health care professional might also suggest that you take other specific homeopathic remedies for discomfort during menopause.

Ayurveda views hot flashes as excess of pitta (the fire element). Women experiencing hot flashes are advised to eliminate or cut down on cayenne, garlic, ginger, onions, and highly acidic foods such as berries, oranges, grapefruits, and tomatoes. It is best to avoid foods that are hot in temperature, as well as hot tubs, very hot baths, saunas, steam baths, and exercise in extreme heat. Drinking alcoholic beverages is believed to aggravate hot flashes in some women.

Practical tips for managing hot flashes may include wiping your face, neck, and upper body with a cool cloth; keeping a change of nightclothes handy; sipping cold water or drinking cold beverages that do not contain caffeine; avoiding long exposure in the hot sun or hot rooms; using fans to keep air circulating in your environment; or taking a break during physical activity that causes your body to overheat.

Lack of Energy

Lack of energy is a common complaint of women during menopause. Generally, as a woman's body changes, it requires additional support and assistance in order to keep it operating efficiently. Good nutritional intake of foods and supplements, adequate rest, relaxation, and stress management are all essential and beneficial during this time of life, especially for women who experience hot flashes and easily become fatigued from disrupted sleep.

Extreme lack of energy may also be a result of reduced levels of testosterone in a woman's body. Although the amount of testosterone produced by the ovaries is very small, it definitely has an energizing effect. HRT that includes testosterone may be suggested by your physician in cases of extreme fatigue.

Unrelated health problems may also cause fatigue. A complete physical examination may indicate the cause.

What Can I Do About Lack of Energy?

Hormone replacement therapy can increase a woman's energy during menopause. It has been shown to reduce the emotional instability that sometimes accompanies menopause and can cause excessive fatigue. HRT also helps to eliminate an inability to fall asleep that is believed to be caused by low serotonin levels in the brain.

Dietary changes, supplemental intake of specific nutrients, exercise, and relaxation techniques can be surprisingly effective ways to enhance energy during menopause, as discussed in Chapter 7.

Nutritional supplements that are known to enhance energy include the following:

- Calcium (1,000 mg) and magnesium (500 mg) at bedtime can help a woman get a good night's sleep, to awaken with more energy the next day.
- If your doctor determines that inadequate thyroid function is a problem, the iodine in sea vegetables such as kelp can be taken in supplemental form.
- If an iron deficiency exists from excessive menstrual bleeding, supplemental intake of iron can help.

- Inadequate adrenal function can contribute to a lack of energy. If that is the case, supplements for hot flashes discussed earlier in this chapter may be helpful.
- Herbs that have a rejuvenating effect in the body, such as bee pollen, gota kola, and alfalfa, can be taken early in the day.

Vaginal Dryness

Vaginal dryness during menopause is directly related to reduced hormone production by the body. The vaginal lining contains glands that secrete fluid when stimulated by hormones produced by the ovaries.

Although vaginal dryness is not a symptom of a more serious condition, it can be disturbing because it makes sexual intercourse uncomfortable. It also occurs during the same period of time when tissue in the vagina becomes thinner and more easily damaged or torn. This can result in vaginal bleeding or an increased likelihood of infection.

What Can I Do About Vaginal Dryness?

Hormone replacement therapy is known to alleviate vaginal dryness. Supplemental use of estrogen and natural progesterone cream inserted in the vagina are also effective. But it's important to realize that the body absorbs hormones applied vaginally or on the skin. Your HRT risk factors must still be considered.

There are numerous supplements and nondrug treatments that can help to alleviate vaginal dryness. The supplements discussed earlier in this chapter, which enhance estrogen production to help alleviate hot flashes, may also reduce vaginal dryness. In addition:

- Vitamin E capsules can be punctured and a few drops inserted into the vagina for lubrication.
- Aloe vera gel can be used as a lubricant. K-Y Jelly and other over-the-counter remedies such as Replens are effective for relief of vaginal dryness.
- Regular sexual activity, either with a partner or alone, also enhances lubrication of the vagina.

Loss of Sexual Desire

Loss of sexual desire during menopause does not usually result from loss of hormone production within the body, although lack of testosterone could cause that effect. Testosterone, the androgen manufactured in small amounts by the ovaries, is sometimes linked to sexual desire. The hormonal and circulatory changes during menopause can also increase sexual arousal time and the need for more stimulation to reach orgasm. Also, vaginal dryness caused by hormonal changes can make sexual intercourse painful, dousing the flames of sexual desire.

Tiredness caused by lack of sleep, poor stress management, or emotional ups and downs can cause you to feel disinterested in sexual interaction. Emotional uncertainty about your self-image as it changes along with your body can result in a hesitancy about sexual intimacy as well.

After menopause has concluded, many women report increased sexual desire, saying their inability to become pregnant is liberating, enabling them to focus mainly on the emotional and sensory feelings of attraction or love for another person.

What Can I Do to Increase My Sexual Desire?

HRT, or the alternatives discussed earlier in this chapter to relieve vaginal dryness, can usually give a woman a general feeling of well-being that enhances her sexual desire. A woman with severe loss of sexual desire can discuss with her doctor the possibility of having her HRT include testosterone.

Nondrug therapies to help restore lost sexual desire during menopause include an overall health-enhancing diet, exercise, and lifestyle changes that are beneficial for the body, mind, and sexuality of a woman. Enhancing your self-image is probably the best aphrodisiac you can find.

Although it is said that specific foods are aphrodisiacs, it has not been proven. Still, foods that will increase the vitality needed for sexual energy include brewer's yeast, broccoli, cantaloupe, carrots, chocolate, cinnamon, eggs, peas, seafood, soy products, and spinach.

Herbs that have been used as sexual stimulants include the following:

- Ginseng is considered a powerful aphrodisiac, although it can be too stimulating for some women to take.
- Yohimbe stimulates testosterone, although it can be detrimental to existing heart, liver, or kidney problems.
- Hops has a powerful estrogen effect in the body, and it is sometimes recommended that hops tea be taken as a sexual stimulant.

- Parsley tea is said to be a mild sexual stimulant.
- A tea made of savory and fenugreek is an old French recipe for sexual stimulation.

Emotional Changes

The reduced production of estrogen and progesterone by the ovaries has an effect on your nervous system and can contribute to emotional changes during menopause in other ways, too. There are two schools of thought about whether estrogen deficiency or progesterone deficiency is responsible for menopausal emotional changes.

Progesterone, in particular, is linked to PMS and is widely used in England for its treatment. Dramatically increased levels of progesterone beginning during the second trimester of pregnancy are said to account for the feeling of euphoria many pregnant women experience.

On the other hand, experts who study brain function and chemistry believe that reduced levels of estrogen in the brain may be a cause of depression and an inability to sleep. Estrogen protects the system in the brain that regulates a neurotransmitter (a substance necessary for effective communication between the nerves in the brain) called serotonin. Studies have shown that serotonin imbalance can lead to depression, obsessive compulsive disorder, increased appetite or hunger, and aggressive behaviors, as well as affect sleep onset.

As in all things, balance is important. One expert characterized hormonally related emotional problems this way: "Estrogen is the body's natural antidepressant and progesterone is the body's natural anti-anxiety and anti-inflammatory."

Besides the physical changes that occur in almost every part of a woman's body during menopause, she may begin to feel and see herself starting to age. It may take time to get used to these changes. You may begin to view your body and your sexuality differently as adjustments in your sex life are made because of vaginal changes.

Sometimes emotional changes during menopause are not related entirely to physical adjustments but are caused by the lifestyle or environmental factors of everyday life. The pressures many women experience during the middle years of life can be difficult to handle emotionally. The stress reduction techniques discussed in Chapter 7 may be helpful when that is the case.

What Can I Do to Stabilize My Emotions?

Emotional changes directly related to diminished hormone production can often be alleviated by HRT. However, some studies have shown that taking estrogen can cause a woman to experience more depressive symptoms.

Unless they are severe, emotional changes alone are usually not a good reason to take HRT.

Some doctors prescribe tranquilizers or antidepressants for a woman who has severe emotional problems during menopause. There are also numerous natural methods for balancing the emotions and relieving anxiety that do not have the side effects of tranquilizers and antidepressants.

Women seeking natural methods to stabilize their emotions may find dietary changes and exercise beneficial. Eliminating stimulating foods or depressants such as sugar, coffee, chocolate, alcohol, and cigarettes has been shown to calm the nerves and balance the emotions.

Supplemental intake of calcium, magnesium, and B-complex vitamins has a calming effect in the body. Herbal teas are effective, including those containing chamomile, passion flower, hops, catnip, skullcap, and peppermint.

Aromatherapy can be extremely calming to the nerves and emotions. Sage eases tension and balances hormones. Chamomile and lavender enhance relaxation and calm nerves. Thyme can alleviate insomnia and improve circulation. Use a few drops of basil, cypress, rosemary, and thyme in a nice, warm bath.

Homeopathic remedies and Bach flower remedies can be especially helpful for emotional changes during menopause. Also extremely beneficial are massage, reflexology, and relaxation techniques and therapies such as biofeedback, guided imagery, hypnotherapy, yoga, dance therapy, listening to music, meditation, and prayer.

Body Aches and Pains

Body aches and pains, general discomfort in the bones, and backaches are common complaints of women during menopause. It is known that the sudden drop in hormones during and after menopause is a catalyst for bone loss, although osteoporosis itself has no real symptoms. Backache, especially in the lower back, can be caused by energy changes in the pelvic organs.

HRT may alleviate some of the aches and pains a woman experiences during menopause.

Dietary adjustments can enhance the rejuvenative abilities of the body and make the work of the digestive system easier and more effective.

Massage, acupuncture, and acupressure are especially beneficial for a woman at this time, and homeopathic remedies can provide relief as well.

A moderate, routine exercise program is beneficial for the body in every way, as discussed in Chapter 7. Women who do not feel up to strenuous activity may select gentle stretching and a type of yoga that is relaxing. Dance therapy can be either relaxing or invigorating. It can be a woman's way of celebrating life, a ritual performed by people throughout the ages in every culture.

Conclusion

The severity of a woman's menopausal symptoms is often a determining factor when deciding whether hormone replacement therapy is her best choice. While HRT does effectively relieve menopausal symptoms in most women, finding a dosage that is effective without causing side effects can sometimes require patience, experimentation, and additional consultations with a physician.

It's important to consider all of your risk factors before deciding whether HRT is a safe choice based on your own health profile and your family health history. The menopausal transition period is a good time to begin thinking about long-term health care choices and lifestyle changes.

Menopausal symptoms can often be reduced and controlled by lifestyle adjustments and alternative and natural health-enhancing methods and programs. Health-enhancing lifestyle changes made before, during, and after menopause are a positive and empowering reflection of your self-esteem and self-image.

Question 3

Can HRT Benefit Me?

Deciding whether HRT can benefit you may seem confusing and frustrating when your life is already filled with unfamiliar physical and emotional changes. A systematic approach can help you make the hormone decision one step at a time.

- Learn about the various kinds of hormones you might take and the pros and cons of each.
- Assess your own health profile, which will show you where the effects and side effects of HRT could be beneficial or detrimental to your immediate and long-term health. It's important to take your health risks seriously.
- Consult a physician and ask for your health to be evaluated with the various laboratory tests and physical examinations detailed in this chapter. Ask for a copy of all your test results to take home and keep in your personal health file.
- Discuss every aspect of your physical condition, your test results, and your treatment choices with your doctor. Ask questions. If your questions cannot be answered to your satisfaction, take your test results to another doctor who will answer your questions.

- Finally, the choice of your own health program is yours alone. You can agree or disagree with any doctor. A doctor's opinions and suggestions can be added to the pool of information you have collected from other sources. Once you have a total picture of your health and health care needs, then you can make an informed decision based on your doctor's opinions, the information you have gathered from your doctor and other sources, and any feelings you have about your own health and medical treatment.

What Do I Need to Know About Hrt and Its Pros and Cons?

The first thing you need to understand is that choosing to take HRT requires a commitment to undergoing regular medical checkups and routine monitoring semiannually and annually, at which time your doctor may suggest that additional tests are needed because of your individual health profile.

Routine semiannual tests and examinations include:

- A blood pressure reading
- A red blood cell count (hemoglobin)
- A blood cholesterol screening, if you have a personal history of high cholesterol or a family history of heart disease
- A clinical breast examination by your physician
- A urinalysis

Routine annual tests and examinations include:

- A pelvic and rectal exam.
- A Pap smear, if you have an intact uterus.

- A mammogram, annually for women over age fifty or for women over age forty who are at high risk for breast cancer. Current American Cancer Society guidelines suggest a mammogram for women between forty and forty-nine every year or two, depending on their personal medical history and risk factors.

In addition, a complete general physical exam is advised at appropriate intervals for women taking HRT, including an EKG (electrocardiogram) for women at high risk for heart disease and a bone scan for women at high risk for osteoporosis.

What Is HRT?

HRT is a physician-prescribed program of treatment for women who are experiencing hormonal imbalances, usually during and after menopause. HRT may consist of estrogen alone (ERT), or estrogen combined with progestins, phytoestrogens, natural progesterone, or testosterone in various combinations (all considered HRT). Each hormone has a different effect in your body.

Estrogen

The estrogens prescribed for women can be either naturally derived or synthetically produced. Estrone and estradiol are the two types of estrogen most often prescribed. Less potent forms of natural estrogen, called phytoestrogens, are derived from plants. Estriol is a phytoestrogen used for HRT.

The brand name Premarin was, before July, 2002, one of the most popular forms of estrogen prescribed for menopausal and postmenopausal women, and it was the second most prescribed medication in the United States. While Premarin may still be a beneficial choice for many women, its reputation—as well as the reputation of all brands of estrogen/progestin HRT—has been tainted by the results of the Women's Health Initiative study, which was abruptly discontinued because it was determined that the health risks for the participants were too great for the study to continue.

Actually, Premarin was somewhat controversial, but for different reasons, before the WHI study results were released. It is described as a natural estrogen because it's manufactured partially from the urine of pregnant mares. However, many alternative health care professionals say that it might be natural to horses, but it's not natural to women.

There has been further controversy surrounding Premarin because of the way it's produced. Female horses raised on "estrogen farms" are kept continually pregnant and confined. After birth, male foals are destroyed because they cannot support the production of urine used to make Premarin. Animal rights activists have campaigned for programs to resolve these conditions, which they consider cruelty. While they have not been successful in changing the conditions under which pregnant mares are housed, they have successfully created male foal adoption programs.

There is a difference between the effects of natural estrogens and synthetic estrogens in a woman's body. Natural estrogens are not as potent as most synthetic estrogens and appear to cause fewer side effects. The most potent synthetic estrogens suppress ovulation and are usually prescribed as birth control pills, not for menopausal and postmenopausal use.

The biggest concern about taking estrogen is the increased risk of breast cancer, which is associated with estrone and estradiol. However, estriol, the weakest form of estrogen, does not increase the risk of cancer and is even believed to protect the body against it.

Women with breast or endometrial cancer are usually advised to avoid estrogen therapy, as are women with breast fibroids, because this estrogen-dependent condition may worsen when estrogen is taken.

How Is Estrogen Taken?

Estrogen can be taken in various ways: orally in pill form; by injection; vaginally through suppositories, creams, or vaginal rings; or absorbed through the skin from patches. Taking estrogen orally is the most common choice of women, probably because it is prescribed by doctors more often and it's easy and convenient. But this form of HRT can have both positive and negative effects.

Oral Estrogen

For oral estrogen to be most effective, it must be adequately absorbed by the intestines and pass through the liver to enter a woman's general circulation. However, some women may not adequately absorb estrogen through the intestines and will need to take higher doses for the estrogen to be effective. Taking more potent doses of oral estrogen may increase its side effects and health risks.

Because oral estrogen passes through the liver, it stimulates the production of proteins that may increase blood pressure, interfere with blood clotting, or negatively affect the gallbladder. Although uncommon, these are documented side effects when oral doses of estrogen are too high for the body to utilize it positively.

Estrogen replacement drugs may lower zinc levels and increase copper levels in the blood. Zinc deficiencies can lead to depression, and copper elevation can increase moodiness.

Estrogen Injections

When a woman is recovering from surgical removal of her ovaries, estrogen injections are often used to prevent hot flashes and other negative effects of her immediate menopause because she can't tolerate oral estrogen. Estrogen injections have the advantage of being absorbed directly into the body's circulation without passing through the stomach, intestines, and liver.

However, there are numerous disadvantages to estrogen injections, the most obvious being the discomfort and inconvenience of the shots. After injection there can be an initial high level of estrogen metabolism by the body, followed by an uncontrollable diminishing supply. If a woman experiences the side effects sometimes associated with estrogen intake there is no way to counteract them, and it may take three or four weeks before they subside. Other forms of estrogen offer a woman better control and quicker withdrawal if she desires it.

Estrogen Cream

The absorption of estrogen vaginally is usually not reliable enough to be considered for estrogen replacement therapy. However, vaginal applications of estrogen can be helpful for women who choose not to take estrogen replacement therapy but still desire the benefits estrogen can offer for vaginal dryness and atrophy.

The needs of every woman differ. For some, a small amount of estrogen cream inserted into the vagina once a week may be enough to relieve dryness; others may require application three times a week. However, estrogen creams are not intended to be substitutes for vaginal lubricants and are not effective for that purpose.

Estrogen cream can be used vaginally along with other types of HRT, but since vaginally applied estrogen is absorbed into the system to some degree, you should discuss your personal treatment program with your physician, including the health risks associated with introducing unopposed estrogen into your body.

Estrogen Patch

Since its development, the estrogen skin patch, such as Estraderm, has usually been used when injections would have been used in the past. The skin patch provides a natural form of estrogen, (17-B estradiol) that enables a woman's body to absorb estrogen without it passing through the stomach, intestines, and liver. Therefore, the risks associated with liver disease, gallbladder disease, high blood pressure, and blood clotting are decreased. Consequently, transdermal application of HRT is becoming more popular, and some women find it easier and more convenient than taking pills. Some women experience skin irritation from wearing the patch, however.

The estrogen skin patch is applied once or twice a week and slowly releases estrogen into the body just as the ovaries would do if they were present or functioning. The patch has been shown to alleviate the discomforts of menopause such as hot flashes and vaginal dryness. It also has been shown to be effective for postmenopausal osteoporosis prevention.

The skin patch only provides estrogen to the body and will not benefit women who select a combination estrogen/progesterone therapy unless an oral progestin or natural progesterone are used at the same time.

Monitoring Your Health

Using estrogen in any form requires regular, periodic monitoring by your physician. If you are uncertain about the effectiveness of your choice of estrogen intake, your doctor may suggest the following laboratory tests:

- Your vaginal estrogen levels can be determined by analyzing a vaginal smear.
- Your blood cholesterol levels can be monitored to assess heart disease risk status.
- Your estrogen blood levels can be monitored to determine if you are absorbing enough estrogen into your circulation.
- Your osteoporosis status and bone loss can be evaluated with periodic bone density measurements.

Progestins and Natural Progesterone

When HRT was first prescribed for women, estrogen alone was the recommended treatment for most menopausal and postmenopausal women. But by the mid-1970s, studies began to indicate that women taking estrogen alone were five times more likely to develop uterine cancer and breast cancer. Subsequent studies showed that taking progestins along with the estrogen for at least ten days each month reduced the incidence of uterine cancer.

The use of progesterone in hormone replacement therapy can restore the natural estrogen/progesterone balance in a woman's body. Because progesterone has a beneficial effect on the uterus, adding progesterone to HRT reduces the risk of endometrial and uterine cancer caused by excessive estrogen. Therefore, women who still have a uterus during and after menopause are advised to add progestins or natural progesterone to their treatment programs when choosing hormone replacement therapy. If a woman's uterus has been removed (hysterectomy), progestins are generally not recommended because they have been shown to have negative side effects.

Progestins can be taken in the same ways as estrogens: orally, vaginally, and by injection.

Some studies indicate that progestins appear to have the opposite effect of estrogen on the HDL-cholesterol levels of the body, causing beneficial cholesterol to be lowered, possibly offsetting the benefits of estrogen against heart disease. Progestins also may increase a woman's risk for breast cancer. Although not as common, other possible side effects of progestins may include anxiety, depression, moodiness, nervousness, headaches, and abdominal bloating.

Progestins taken with estrogen cyclically simulate the natural rise and fall of hormones in the menstrual cycle before menopause and may cause a return of monthly menstrual bleeding. This side effect can be eliminated with lower doses of progestins or by taking progestins every two or three months, rather than monthly on a cyclical schedule.

Progestins have been shown to relieve hot flashes for women who cannot take estrogen because they have medical conditions that would be exacerbated by estrogen intake. However, women taking progestins alone cannot count on improvement of vaginal dryness or protection against heart disease.

When progestins were first added to estrogen in HRT, they were derived from the hormones testosterone and 19-nortestosterone. Although they are still prescribed, these progestational agents may have an androgenic effect in women, resulting in masculine-like symptoms such as weight gain and muscle development, oily skin and acne, unwanted hair growth, lowering of the voice, and enlargement of the clitoris. Stronger doses may also have a more negative effect on blood cholesterol levels, increasing the risk of heart disease.

Progestins derived from testosterone are often used in birth control pills along with estrogen. The progesterone-only birth control pills (Micronor and Ovrette) prescribed for women who cannot take estrogen contain testosterone derivatives, as does levonorgestrel, the hormone used in Norplant, the contraceptive implant.

The testosterone-derived progestin norethindrone is being used for postmenopausal treatment because the lower dosage has been shown to cause fewer side effects.

What Is the Difference Between Natural Progesterone and Progestins?

Natural progesterone is identical in molecular structure to the progesterone manufactured by the body. Progestins are synthetically produced by modifying the molecular structure of progesterone derived from plants or from testosterone. Once the progesterone molecule is synthetically altered in a laboratory, it becomes a progestin and is no longer considered natural progesterone. Therefore, the distinction between natural progesterone and progestins is important when discussing and considering HRT.

Because natural progesterone is identical in molecular structure to progesterone produced by the body, it performs the same role within the body's complicated hormonal interaction. Progestins do not all have the same effects in the body.

For the purposes of HRT, both have the same beneficial effect on the endometrium, protecting the uterine lining and possibly triggering menstrual flow. But each may also cause menstrual periods to return or periodic spotting or breakthrough bleeding to occur. Natural progesterone may increase thyroid activity somewhat, a possible concern for women who take thyroid medication. However, progestins have known side effects within the body that natural progesterone does not appear to have. For these reasons, the use of natural progesterone as HRT has recently become more popular.

Natural progesterone can be taken orally, supplied to the body transdermally by massaging a cream containing diosgenin into the skin, or sublingually by holding a vitamin E oil–based diosgenin under the tongue.

A common treatment of PMS before menopause, natural progesterone can be used alone during premenopause when a woman's body may have excessive estrogen effects. After menopause, it is usually used with an estrogen.

Advocates of natural progesterone have found it to be very effective in relieving both PMS and the discomforts of menopause, to reduce the risk of other serious health conditions that women develop after menopause, such as heart disease and osteoporosis, and to stimulate formation of new bone in women with osteoporosis.

Natural progesterone HRT is a fairly recent development. Most doctors are more familiar with progestins because they learn about them in medical school and because the large drug companies promote the use of their products that contain progestins. However, the benefits of natural progesterone are beginning to be more widely recognized by physicians.

At this time, medical documentation of the use of natural progesterone is considered anecdotal, because it is being used without double-blind studies for comparison (although studies are being undertaken at this time). Scientifically designed studies usually result for two reasons. Before a drug can be approved by the Food and Drug Administration (FDA) for general use, it must undergo extensive scientific medical study. After FDA approval, many drug companies underwrite usage studies in order to promote the sale of their products.

Because the molecular structure of natural progesterone is not altered, it is considered a natural substance, not a drug. It cannot be patented by drug companies and no prescription is required for the purchase of natural progesterone creams and oral suspension. As a result, extensive drug testing has not been done using natural progesterone for the purpose of FDA approval, and there is no benefit for drug companies to underwrite studies to promote a product they cannot patent and which can be easily produced by others.

Your doctor can prescribe an estrogen/natural progesterone combination HRT derived from plant sources. The oral form contains natural progesterone with tri-estrogen, which is 80 percent estriol (phytoestrogen), 10 percent estrone, and 10 percent estradiol. A phytoestrogen/natural progesterone cream (OstaDerm) and gel are also available for topical or vaginal application. (Often this prescription is taken to a "formulating pharmacy"; therefore, your prescribing doctor may need to tell you where to have your prescription filled.)

A phytoestrogen/natural progesterone cream or gel is applied to the skin, usually on the stomach, until menopausal discomfort stops. It can be used the entire month, if necessary, except the last four or five days. It can also be inserted vaginally.

For women who prefer a more natural and gentle approach to their menopausal health care, the tri-estrogen/natural progesterone combination has been shown to be effective in relieving a woman's menopausal discomforts while it reduces her risk of cancer and protects her bone health.

A woman who has taken Premarin and/or Provera and has experienced side effects may elect to switch to the phytoestrogen/natural progesterone combination.

Although the use of natural progesterone and phytoestrogen/natural progesterone HRT is increasing every day, many doctors may still be unfamiliar with them because their use is not promoted by large drug companies. Doctors who seek to offer alternative or combination conventional/alternative treatment programs are more likely to be familiar with the natural hormones, their uses, and their benefits. The Resources section provides sources for information on the natural hormones that you may wish to share with your doctor.

Testosterone

Testosterone is generally considered a male hormone because it is abundantly produced by the bodies of men; however, a small quantity of testosterone is also produced by the ovaries of women. This small amount released prior to menopause appears to influence the energy level and sex drive of women. When testosterone is added to estrogen in HRT it seems to have that same function in menopausal and postmenopausal women, adding to a feeling of well-being and potentially increasing their sex drive.

Because testosterone does not protect the uterine lining, as natural progesterone or progestins do, it is not prescribed as HRT in place of progestins for a woman whose uterus is intact. A woman who has had a hysterectomy may be advised to take a testosterone/estrogen combination during and after menopause.

Testosterone can be taken orally in tablet form or applied to the body as a cream. Recently the use of testosterone cream to increase sexual stimulation in menopausal women has become popular. However, it's important to remember that testosterone can have a masculinizing effect on women unless used in minute amounts. Other side effects of the use of testosterone cream have not been determined. It is best to discuss testosterone cream with your physician before experimenting with it.

Taking Hormones

HRT may be taken in a cycle or continuously. Cyclic HRT can be taken in two ways. In the first, estrogen alone is taken during the first twelve days of the month, then, beginning the thirteenth day, progestin or natural progesterone is taken along with estrogen through the twenty-fifth day of the month. Finally, no medication is taken for the rest of the month, which duplicates a woman's normal menstrual cycle.

However, some women experience headaches and hot flashes during the five or six days they do not take the estrogen. If this happens, a woman may choose to take estrogen every day of the month, with a progestin or natural progesterone added for ten to thirteen days each month, usually at the beginning of the month.

For a woman who can take estrogen and who chooses to do so, it is important to add a progestin or natural progesterone for a period of time during the month to protect the uterine lining if her uterus is intact.

Most women with an intact uterus who are taking cyclic HRT still have menstrual periods, even after menopause, because the sudden drop in the progestin or natural progesterone causes shedding of the uterine lining. However, their periods will probably be lighter than before and will gradually decrease over time. To eliminate this side effect of cyclic HRT, some women may prefer continuous HRT.

Continuous HRT can be taken in two ways. A woman takes estrogen plus a very low dosage of a progestin every day of the month or she takes the estrogen/progestin combination five days a week, with weekends off.

Continuous HRT can eliminate the menstrual bleeding many women find undesirable after menopause. It protects the uterine lining with lower doses of progestins than those usually required in cyclic therapy. When breakthrough bleeding still occurs, an adjustment in the progestin dosage may be needed until the right balance is achieved.

Although lower levels of progestins may be taken during continuous HRT, progestins may still have a negative effect on blood cholesterol levels and increase the risk of heart disease.

Until the completion of menopause a woman's ovaries are still producing hormones to some degree, often irregularly, making it difficult to regulate HRT intake. Therefore, women who have completed menopause generally find continuous HRT more comfortable and beneficial.

What Factors Do My Doctor and I Need to Consider When Assessing My Health Profile?

It is very important to inform your doctor completely about your personal and genetic family medical history, what medical treatments you are currently receiving, and any current symptoms and the length of time you have been experiencing them. These will indicate what medical conditions you may currently have, whether menopause is a possibility for you, and if it is, what stage of menopause you may have reached.

The entire medical history of you and your family is very important when considering HRT. Genetic predisposition to certain disorders and diseases, such as breast cancer, uterine cancer, heart disease, osteoporosis, and diabetes, may make it risky or even dangerous for some women to take HRT.

Your doctor will need to know:

- About any medical treatment you are currently receiving
- Your current and recent physical complaints and symptoms
- What medications you are currently taking (including over-the-counter pain relievers, antacids, and cold remedies) or have taken in the past
- Any nutritional supplements, herbs, and nondrug remedies you have recently taken or are currently taking
- Your sexual habits and lifestyle patterns, including nutritional intake, smoking, and alcohol consumption

You must be completely honest with your doctor so that a realistic treatment program can be suggested and discussed with you. Make notes ahead of time of your medications and supplements, physical complaints, and symptoms. While no complaint or symptom is too incidental, heart palpitations and bone discomfort are especially important. Take your notes with you to the doctor's office, because sometimes it is difficult to remember everything you want to tell the doctor once you're there. You may want to save these notes in a personal health file you keep at home.

Based on this information, your doctor will conduct a complete physical examination to determine your overall health status and risk factors. If menopause is a factor in your health care, your doctor can evaluate the hormone levels and production in your body during your physical exam and after a variety of laboratory tests.

What Examination and Tests Will My Doctor Want Me to Have?

You need a complete general physical examination so your doctor can assess your overall health and suggest appropriate treatments or preventive measures. The exam will include a blood pressure reading, gynecological and pelvic exam, Pap smear to determine if your cervical cells are normal, and, perhaps, a maturation index to measure the estrogen effect in your vagina. A progesterone challenge or endometrial biopsy may be needed if you have a personal history of endometriosis or irregular uterine bleeding.

Laboratory tests are also important, as follows:

- A urinalysis to see if you're pregnant and to determine if your kidneys, bladder, and liver are functioning properly and are free of infection.
- Blood will be drawn and sent to a laboratory for:
    - A complete blood count to determine if you have a healthy number of red and white blood cells, which will indicate, among other things, if you have developed anemia from excessive menstrual bleeding.
    - A blood chemistry test to analyze the chemicals in your blood, which will show if you have normal levels of minerals and other elements, giving your doctor an idea of your overall health.

- An analysis of your blood-clotting factors, especially important if you have a personal or family history of blood-clotting disorders or disease.
- A cholesterol count to determine if your levels are normal, an indication of cardiovascular and heart disease risk. (Ask to have your cholesterol count include total cholesterol, HDL, LDL, and triglyceride levels.)
- Fasting blood sugar levels if you have a personal or family history of diabetes or hypoglycemia.
- A kidney function test.
- A liver function test, important if you are considering HRT in pill form because the hormones will pass through the liver before entering your circulation.
- A thyroid function test, because HRT effectiveness in your body can be affected by thyroid function, and your thyroid function can be affected by HRT.
- A test for syphilis and possibly HIV (human immunodeficiency virus).

Your doctor may also ask you to see a radiologist for additional health evaluation. A radiologist uses advanced medical detection machines to assess the condition of your breasts, pelvic organs, and bones with these tests:

- A mammogram to determine if your breast tissue is normal and healthy. The results will also be compared to your baseline mammogram if you've had one previously. If you have not, this one will become your baseline for future comparisons. A mammogram is especially important if you have a personal or genetic family history of breast irregularities or cancer.

- A bone scan would be appropriate if you have had bone discomfort, fractures, or a personal or family history of osteoporosis. It will be compared to your baseline if you've had previous bone scans or will become your baseline for future scans.
- A pelvic ultrasound if your physical exam or your symptoms indicate you may have abnormalities of your uterus, endometrium (lining of the uterus), or ovaries.
- An electrocardiogram (EKG) is not routinely performed on women during menopause; however, it is important to ask for one if your genetic family history indicates cardiovascular disease or heart attacks at an early age. An EKG is very important if you routinely experience heart palpitations or discomfort in your chest and stomach that you dismiss as indigestion.

Your doctor may also want to have tests conducted to determine your body's hormone levels. These tests may include:

- A maturation index of cells taken from your vaginal lining—similar to a Pap smear of the cervix—will indicate the effect of estrogen on your vaginal tissues. The quantity of three types of vaginal cells is observed under a microscope: superficial cells, parabasal cells, and basal cells. A majority of parabasal cells indicates little stimulation of the vaginal tissue by estrogen and usually means menopause.
- Hormone blood levels will be measured from your blood sample. If estrogen levels in your blood are low, it may indicate menopause, especially when your FSH (follicle-stimulating hormone) level is high. FSH is a hormone released by the hypothalamus and pituitary glands of the brain in the complicated interaction between them and the ovaries. FSH and LH

(luteinizing hormone) stimulate the ovarian follicles to ripen and release eggs. When ovarian follicles cannot produce enough estrogen to release an egg, a message is sent to the hypothalamus and pituitary glands. They, in turn, release more FSH, sending a return message to stimulate the ovaries into producing estrogen. When the ovaries are not able to produce enough estrogen to release an egg, the FSH level in the blood will be high and estrogen levels low, usually indicating menopause.

When your doctor discusses your test results with you, either over the phone or during another office consultation, don't be shy about asking questions about your results at this time, or about calling the doctor later with follow-up questions.

Few doctors offer to give you copies of your test results. However, you are entitled to have copies, which you may want to keep in your own personal health file at home.

Conclusion

Determining whether HRT might benefit you requires evaluation by a doctor of your medical records and medical history, a thorough physical examination, and laboratory testing. Only then can your current overall health status and potential health risks be evaluated realistically.

Women who experience extremely debilitating discomfort or distress from hot flashes, vaginal dryness, and emotional instability during menopause have reported significant relief from HRT. Women who are at high risk of developing osteoporosis or colon cancer are often encouraged to take HRT.

Once your risk factors have been determined, the decision to take HRT or not is entirely yours to make. The following summary of the various kinds of HRT may help you make that decision.

Estrogen/Progestin HRT
(such as Prempro, which was used in the WHI study)

You might want to consider this therapy if you have an intact uterus.

Short-term benefits: Can provide relief for menopausal physical and emotional discomfort and distress by alleviating hot flashes, smoothing out mood swings and emotional irritability, aiding sleep, and relieving vaginal dryness.

Long-term benefits: Can relieve vaginal dryness, help to maintain healthy pelvic organs, help to maintain skin elasticity and healthy hair, may improve memory and concentration, contributes to the prevention of osteoporosis, reduces hip fractures, and reduces incidence of colon cancer.

The experts say . . .

- A woman who is still producing hormones, even low levels, and is not experiencing any significant discomfort associated with menopause usually is not advised to start HRT, unless she is at extreme risk for osteoporosis or colon cancer.
- Women with a history of endometrial disorders or breast problems, including breast fibroids, are usually advised to avoid HRT that includes estrogen.

- Women who have or have had breast or uterine cancer should avoid estrogen.
- Progestins taken with estrogen cyclically simulate the natural rise and fall of hormones in the menstrual cycle before menopause and may cause a return of monthly menstrual bleeding. This side effect can be eliminated with lower doses of progestins or by taking progestins every two or three months, rather than monthly on a cyclical schedule.

Estrogen Alone

You might want to consider this if you have had a hysterectomy.

Short-term benefits: Can provide relief for menopausal physical and emotional discomfort and distress by alleviating hot flashes, smoothing out mood swings and emotional irritability, aiding sleep, and relieving vaginal dryness.

Long-term benefits: Can relieve vaginal dryness, help to maintain healthy pelvic organs, help to maintain skin elasticity and healthy hair, may improve memory and concentration, contributes to the prevention of osteoporosis, reduces hip fractures, reduces incidence of colon cancer.

The experts say . . .

- Women with a history of endometrial disorders or breast problems, including breast fibroids, are usually advised to avoid HRT that includes estrogen.

- Women who have or have had breast or uterine cancer should avoid estrogen.
- The experts are undecided on heart disease, stroke, and blood-clot risks, but for now it appears it is safe for women without a uterus to take unopposed estrogen.

Progestins Alone

You might want to consider this if you cannot take estrogen.

Short-term benefits: Can relieve hot flashes; however, taking progestins alone usually doesn't improve vaginal dryness.

The experts say . . .

- Some progestins appear to increase LDL-cholesterol levels in the body, causing beneficial cholesterol to be lowered, thereby increasing heart disease.
- Progestins may increase anxiety, depression, moodiness, nervousness, headaches, and abdominal bloating.

Natural Progesterone

You might want to consider this type of therapy if you have an intact uterus.

Short-term benefits: Provides relief for menopausal physical and emotional discomfort and distress by alleviating hot flashes, smoothing out mood swings and emotional irritability, aiding sleep, and relieving vaginal dryness.

Long-term benefits: Helps skin maintain moisture and elasticity, protects the uterus, and reduces the risk of developing osteoporosis. For treatment of osteoporosis, natural progesterone stimulates formation of new bone when combined with a healthy diet.

After menopause, natural progesterone is usually used with an estrogen, often a natural tri-estrogen or phytoestrogen (the milder plant-derived estrogen).

The experts say . . .

- While natural progesterone has a beneficial effect on the endometrium, protecting the uterine lining, it may cause menstrual periods to return or periodic spotting or breakthrough bleeding to occur. This effect will usually diminish over time.
- It may increase thyroid activity somewhat, a possible concern for women who take thyroid medication.

Testosterone

Possible benefits: Usually increases sex drive, particularly after the ovaries have been surgically removed; can increase energy; when added to estrogen, can result in a feeling of well-being if the dosage is correct.

The experts say . . .

- A dosage that is too strong can cause agitation, depression, facial hair growth, muscle weight gain, acne, and other masculinizing effects.
- Recently the use of testosterone cream to increase sexual stimulation in women has become popular. However, it's important to remember that testosterone can have a masculinizing effect on women unless used in minute amounts. The side effects of the use of testosterone cream have not been determined. It is best to discuss testosterone cream with your physician before experimenting with it.
- The safety of long-term use of testosterone has not been determined.

Question 4

Is HRT Too Risky to Consider?

Many women are wondering, "Does taking estrogen cause breast cancer?"

Estrogen is known to stimulate all the cells in the body, especially those in the breasts. Although it does not cause cancer, it may promote the growth of cancer cells that already exist within a woman's body or of cancer cells that may develop while a woman is taking HRT.

Many studies, including the latest Women's Health Initiative (WHI) study, whose results were released in July 2002, have established a link between estrogen/progestin HRT and an increased risk of breast cancer. A woman with a personal history of breast problems is usually advised not to take HRT. A woman with an intense fear of breast cancer may elect not to take HRT unless the benefits strongly outweigh her anxiety created by the fear.

Whether taking any of the various kinds of HRT increases a woman's chances of developing breast cancer is controversial. The WHI study, involving postmenopausal women with an intact uterus taking Prempro, one of the estrogen/progestin HRTs on the market, was stopped because the participants' increased risks of developing breast cancer, heart disease, or blood clots, or having a stroke were determined to be too great for the study to continue. But the study that was stopped has a WHI companion study involving women who have had hysterectomies and are taking estrogen without progestins. And that study continues. Although no one has said so, one conclusion that may be assumed, because the first study was stopped and the second study was not, is that it must be safe for women who have had hysterectomies to take unopposed estrogen.

This is not the first time clinical medical studies have sent mixed messages to the consuming public. Why do some studies conclude one thing and others say something else? The types and dosages of hormones taken, as well as the length of time they are taken, seem to be the varying factors in the studies, as are the health profiles of the individual participants. This makes it even more confusing for women who are trying to decide whether HRT is too risky to consider.

Depending on a woman's personal risk factors, the best data available right now indicates that long-term use of estrogen/progestin HRT in moderately high doses increases a woman's risk of developing breast cancer. Lower doses for a short period of time—to relieve severe discomfort or distress during the menopausal transition—seem to carry less risk.

What is known about taking estrogen alone is that some types of estrogen appear to be potentially more harmful than others. The potent dosages of estradiol are confirmed by most studies to significantly increase a woman's breast cancer risk. This may be why estradiol is not widely used in the United States. The naturally derived tri-estrogen and phytoestrogens (plant-derived estrogen) are considered to have a lower breast cancer risk. Most of the other estrogens prescribed as HRT fall somewhere in between.

The three forms of estrogen active in a woman's body are estradiol, estrone, and estriol. Estradiol is the primary estrogen the ovaries produce and is converted into estrone by the intestines. Estriol is produced in large amounts by a woman's body during pregnancy. This leads researchers to believe that there is a connection between progesterone production by the body (which is known to dramatically increase during pregnancy) and the production of estriol. Progesterone production by the ovaries usually stops before estrogen production does during the early years of menopause, resulting in irregular menstrual cycles. This leaves the body out of balance, with more estrogen. Experts agree almost unanimously that one primary reason for breast problems is excessive estrogen's effect on the breasts.

What Effects Do the Different Types of Estrogen HRT Have In a Woman's Body?

The conjugated estrogens in Prempro are converted mostly to estrone in the intestinal tract, mimicking the way the body works naturally before menopause. Estriol (plant-derived) is the mildest form of natural estrogen prescribed for HRT. Although estriol is widely used in Europe without problems, it has not undergone the scientific blind studies considered proof of its overall effectiveness and safety in the United States. Often it does not have the same immediate results for relieving the discomforts of menopause when given in the same dosages as other types of estrogen. Prempro, estrogen/progestin HRT, will usually alleviate hot flashes when taken in dosages of 0.6 to 1.25 mg; however, estriol usually needs to be taken in dosages of 2 to 4 mg to have the same effect.

The higher dosage requirements of estriol are a cause of concern for many physicians. Also, it is not known if estriol has the same beneficial effects as other types of estrogen on a woman's bone health.

Studies conducted twenty-five years ago using estriol showed that it inhibited breast cancer in mice. It was also discovered in a 1966 study that women with breast cancer had high levels of estrone and estradiol in their urine but low levels of estriol, while women without breast cancer had higher estriol levels. In a study, published in the *Journal of the American Medical Association* in 1978, estriol was given to postmenopausal women with breast cancer and 37 percent experienced an improvement in their cancer.

Still, with the recent WHI study having some surprising results, it makes us wonder which studies to believe. Women with some risk of breast cancer face the difficult task of deciding if taking estrogen, whether it's combined with progestin or natural progesterone or not, is worth the risk.

HRT and Breast Cancer

What Are My Risks of Developing Breast Cancer?

There appears to be a genetic predisposition to breast cancer, so a woman whose female blood relatives have had breast cancer needs to be more cautious about taking HRT, especially a woman whose mother or sister experienced breast cancer in both breasts before menopause. This is considered hereditary breast cancer.

Hormonal factors that may influence a woman's risk of developing breast cancer include:

- Menstruation onset at an early age. Studies have shown that women who had their first menstrual period before the age of twelve have twice the risk of breast cancer than women who started menstruating at age thirteen or later.

- Menopause at a later age. Women who have their last menstrual period at age forty-five have half the risk of developing breast cancer as women who enter menopause after age fifty-five.
- Number of years your menstrual cycles are active. Women with thirty years of regular, active menstruation have half the risk of developing breast cancer compared to women who have regular, active menstruation for forty years or longer.

A woman's age, the conditions of her breasts, and her body fat may also be factors, as detailed in the following:

- Breast cancer usually occurs in women over forty, possibly because after that age hormone levels change in the body, often resulting in excessive estrogen effect on the breasts.
- Being overweight after menopause. Although excess body fat in women younger than age fifty does not appear to affect their risk of breast cancer, women over age sixty with excess body fat have as much as an 80 percent greater chance of developing breast cancer. Although the reasons are unclear, this may be related to the fact that the body converts androgens (male hormones) in body fat to estrogen after menopause.
- Women with dense breast tissue are more likely to develop breast cancer. A mammogram is necessary to determine whether your breast tissue is dense.
- A personal history of fibrocysts in the breasts may increase a woman's chance of developing breast cancer, because fibrocysts are believed to result from excessive estrogen effect on breast tissue.

Childbearing also appears to be a factor in a woman's breast cancer risk:

- Women who have never had children have a higher risk of developing breast cancer.
- A woman giving birth to her first child later in life, after the age of thirty, is at higher risk of developing breast cancer than one whose first child was born when she was twenty or younger.
- Women who breast-feed their first child for at least six months appear to have a lower risk of developing breast cancer.

Women who smoke cigarettes and regularly drink alcoholic beverages are at higher risk of developing breast cancer. This may be related to the negative effects of these substances on the liver, which is responsible for metabolizing estrogen so that excess hormones can be excreted from the body instead of being stored in the tissues.

Studies have shown that exposure to environmental toxins such as pesticides, especially DDT, increases a woman's risk of breast cancer. Although the use of DDT was banned in 1972, DDT can be stored in the fatty tissues of the body for decades. Chemicals similar to DDT that are chlorine based are still used as pesticides and in various other ways, such as in disinfectants for swimming pools and in spot removers.

Artificial menopause due to surgical removal of the ovaries reduces a woman's risk of breast cancer.

Assessing Your Breast Cancer Risk Factors

Some women appear to be genetically disposed to developing certain types of breast cancer. That's why it's so important to give a complete medical history of both sides of your family to your doctor when deciding whether to take HRT.

Hereditary breast cancer occurs earlier in life, with the average age being forty-four, as compared to sixty or over for other women.

Hereditary breast cancer involves both breasts in about 46 percent of cases. Women having hereditary breast cancer are at higher risk for developing other cancers such as ovarian, brain, lung, colon, adrenal gland, thyroid, and leukemia.

A woman with a parent or sibling with breast cancer falls into the highest-risk category. A woman with maternal or paternal grandparents, aunts, or uncles with cancer is also considered at risk, although the risk is not as high.

It's important for all women to be concerned about detecting breast changes, especially while taking HRT and in the years just before menopause when breast cancer is more likely to occur. Breast cancer is one of the most successfully treated forms of cancer. Early detection is the key.

Committing to three routine breast examinations gives you the best chance of detecting breast problems as early as possible:

- A monthly self-examination of your breasts.
- A breast physical examination by a health care professional at least once a year, or more often for women who fall into a high-risk category or those with a history of breast problems.
- Mammograms on a regular basis. The American Cancer Society suggests a woman have mammograms as follows:
  - A woman with a high incidence of breast cancer in direct female blood relatives may choose to have her first mammogram as early as age twenty-five. At the very least, she needs to discuss this with her physician.
  - A woman between ages thirty-five and forty who has not

already done so needs to have a mammogram done to serve as a baseline for comparison of all future mammograms, as well as for detection of early breast cancer.

- A woman between ages forty and forty-nine is advised to have a mammogram every one or two years, depending on her personal medical history and risk factors.
- A woman is advised to have a mammogram once a year when she is over age fifty or if she is over age forty and falls into a high-risk category for breast cancer.

A woman taking HRT needs to have her breasts routinely examined by her physician during her annual physical checkup. Because small lumps within the breasts can easily be missed during this exam if it is rushed, make sure your doctor takes the time to be thorough.

Whenever a woman detects breast changes of any kind during a breast self-exam, an additional physician breast exam is absolutely necessary and needs to be performed as soon as possible.

Every woman needs to perform a breast self-examination at least once a month. Often a breast lump is found by a woman herself, not by her physician. Although early cancer is usually painless, while other types of breast problems, such as fibrocysts, are painful to the touch, any lump a woman discovers in her breasts or in her armpits needs to be reported to her physician immediately.

It is best to schedule routine breast self-exams with yourself on a date that is easily remembered, such as the first or last day of the month. If you are on cyclic HRT and have found a routine change in your breasts during the month, you may want to examine yourself two times a month: at a time when your breasts feel unaffected by the hormones, and during the time when the breasts are routinely reacting to the hormones.

Women taking cyclic HRT, as described in Chapter 3, may see or feel slight changes in their breasts during the month similar to the natural cyclic release of hormones by the ovaries. These effects vary depending on the type and dosage of hormones taken.

Breast reactions while taking HRT may be considered routine when they occur at the same time every month, with some women on HRT experiencing general breast tenderness and sensitivity or a slight swelling of the breasts all the time.

If you notice breast changes when you first start taking HRT, it is always best to discuss these changes with your physician. An adjustment in your type of HRT or your dosage may be needed.

Breast Self-Exam

When doing her monthly breast self-exam a woman needs to look at her breasts as well as feel them.

Standing before a mirror, look to see if the size, color, or shape of your breasts has changed in any way, if either breast has taken on a shape different from the other, if there are any obvious lumps or areas of thickened breast tissue, or if there is any crustiness or scaliness on your breasts, especially around the nipples. Raise your hands over your head and look to see if your nipples are inverted or if your breasts have developed any new dimples. If any of these changes or conditions exist, it is necessary to consult your physician right away.

After examining your breasts in the mirror, lie down on a bed to feel for lumps in your breasts. Applying a little oil to your breast during this procedure can make it more comfortable.

Examine one breast at a time, folding the arm on the same side of your body over your head to flatten the breast as much as possible.

Using the pads of the fingers on your opposite hand, slowly make small circular motions around your breast, beginning at the nipple and working outward, covering the entire breast. Feel your breasts for lumps that are harder than normal breast tissue or lumps that do not move freely when you touch them.

Then move to your armpit. You may feel lymph nodes that are normally soft, move freely, and are not painful. If your lymph nodes are firm and do not move freely, report this as well as any suspicious lumps in your breasts to your physician immediately. Finally, gently squeeze each nipple to see if there is any blood or fluid discharge. A pink, bloody, clear yellow, or watery discharge needs to be reported to your physician as soon as possible. A slight milky discharge can be caused by medications you are taking or from childbirth, even years earlier. Still, report it to your physician.

Do My Breasts Feel Abnormal?

Very often the lumps a woman finds during a breast self-exam are fibrocysts, not cancer. Usually, lumps that are harder than normal breast tissue and do not move freely are more suspicious. However, it is always best to report any breast changes or lumps to your doctor. While approximately 10 percent of women develop breast cancer, as many as 40 to 60 percent experience fibrocystic breasts.

Fibrocysts of the breast is a broad term that refers to approximately fifty different benign breast conditions. When a woman's breast feels lumpy and it is referred to as cystic, she may also be told she has fibrocystic breast disease, although it isn't really a disease. Some fibrocysts are simply variations of normal breast tissue, but others are more suspicious and deserve closer attention. In true cystic breast disease, a cyst in a woman's breast becomes prominent and fills with fluid. Cysts are often accompanied by breast tenderness, and some women experience intense pain from fibrocysts.

Some studies say fibrocysts do not turn into breast cancer, while others say women with fibrocysts have a two-to-five-times greater risk of developing breast cancer.

What Should Be Done If I Have Fibrocysts in My Breasts?

Usually, a physician will suggest that a lump of any kind be biopsied to determine that is not cancer. Once it is determined that a lump is a fibrocyst, the treatment can include several approachs. Hormones may be suggested to balance the estrogen and progesterone effects on the breast. Diuretics may be advised because fibrocysts often are filled with fluid. Pain medication can offer relief when the fibrocysts are extremely painful, and dietary changes are usually suggested.

Caffeine and chocolate intake have been linked to fibrocysts of the breast. Coffee, some tea, cola drinks with caffeine, and chocolate contain substances belonging to a family of chemicals called methylxanthines. Studies have shown that totally eliminating products containing these chemicals will usually eliminate fibrocysts of the breasts. Cutting down on foods and beverages containing these chemicals is not enough; they need to be completely eliminated from the diet. Once the fibrocysts clear up, if a woman starts to eat and drink these foods and beverages again, the condition usually returns. However, there can be side effects when suddenly stopping caffeine intake altogether, particularly headaches, so taper off before stopping.

A high-fat diet has been associated with fibrocysts of the breast by increasing body fat. Androgens in body fat are converted to estrogen by the body, contributing to an estrogen-progesterone imbalance and increasing the estrogen effect on the breasts.

Studies show that intake of 600 IU of vitamin E daily, along with B complex and the trace mineral selenium, results in an improvement in fibrocystic breast problems in 75 percent of women.

Can My Diet Increase My Risk of Breast Cancer?

Breast cancer appears to develop in stages over a number of years and may be influenced by diet, especially intake of saturated fats. Studies of the correlation between dietary fat intake and breast cancer have led to the conclusion that a high–saturated fat diet increases a woman's risk of developing breast cancer and causes existing breast cancer to be more difficult to control.

It has been reported that a diet high in saturated fat seems to contribute to benign (noncancerous) breast tumors changing to cancer. Active breast cancer has been shown to grow faster and spread farther in women with a high-fat diet, especially older women.

The foods highest in saturated fat include animal fats contained in meat, high-fat cheeses, whole milk, butter, coconut oil, and any fat that is solid at room temperature.

Numerous studies have shown that various dietary factors affect a woman's chances of developing breast cancer:

- In 1991, the *International Journal of Cancer* advised that a high intake of dietary fiber, vitamin C, and beta carotene decreases a woman's risk of postmenopausal breast cancer.
- Other studies have concluded that low thyroid activity due to inadequate dietary intake of iodine can increase a woman's

risk of developing breast cancer. Women who live in Japan and Iceland, where iodine is adequately consumed in seafood and seaweed, have a lower incidence of breast cancer.

- Women with cancer have lower-than-normal blood levels of the trace mineral selenium. Soil with low levels of selenium correlate to areas of the world where women have the highest cancer incidence. However, selenium can be toxic when taken in excess, with no more than 200 mcg daily being the upper limit of intake.
- Because a woman's liver function affects metabolism of estrogen in the body, healthy liver activity is said to reduce a woman's risk of breast cancer. Liver activity may be enhanced with adequate intake of B-complex vitamins, vitamin C, and the trace minerals zinc, copper, manganese, and selenium.
- Specific foods can reduce the body's sensitivity to carcinogens, including cruciferous vegetables such as broccoli, cabbage, and cauliflower. These are believed to have anti–breast cancer elements, called phytochemical indole-3-carbinol (I3C), which deactivate estrogens that stimulate the growth of breast cancer.

HRT and Heart Disease, Blood Clots, and Strokes

Does Taking Hrt Cause Heart Disease, Blood Clots, and Strokes?

The most surprising conclusion that was reached during the discontinued WHI study of Prempro, the estrogen/progestin HRT, and one of the reasons the study was stopped, was that the HRT increased the participants' risks of heart attacks, blood clots, and strokes. It had been assumed for some time that HRT actually prevented heart attacks; blood clots and strokes were a matter of concern. Then we learned that there was another study being conducted at the WHI, a companion study using estrogen alone, involving women who have had hysterectomies. The ongoing results of that study indicate that it's safe to continue until 2005, the planned completion date for both studies. The news that the unopposed estrogen study was not stopped early is reassuring for many women who have been taking unopposed estrogen for a long time.

What do the two studies really tell us? Apparently estrogen can be beneficial to the cardiovascular health of a woman after menopause by lowering her blood cholesterol; however, taking a progestin along with estrogen increases the risks of developing heart disease, blood clots, or having strokes, as well as developing breast cancer.

Studies in the past have indicated that the longer a woman takes estrogen (without progestins), the more it reduces her risk of cardiovascular disease by positively affecting her blood cholesterol levels. Estrogen is also believed to relax the blood vessels, easing heart function.

Estrogen has been shown to raise the levels of HDL (high-density lipoprotein), good cholesterol, in the blood while lowering LDL (low-density lipoprotein), bad cholesterol. HDL collects fat and cholesterol in the blood within envelopes, which allows them to be carried out of the bloodstream, instead of breaking down and being deposited on the artery walls. LDL breaks down more easily, depositing fat on artery walls.

Results of previous studies were also confirmed by the conclusions of the WHI estrogen/progestin study that progestins are generally believed to diminish the positive effects of estrogen on the cardiovascular system. Although the reasons for this are not clear, progestins can contribute to sodium retention in some women, possibly leading to hypertension. Thus, a woman without an intact uterus who takes HRT is prescribed unopposed estrogen (estrogen without progestins), as the progestins are needed primarily to protect the uterus.

Proponents of natural progesterone, as opposed to progestins, say that it is protective against high blood pressure because it has a natural diuretic effect on the body, reducing fluid retention. Natural progesterone is also said to normalize blood clotting.

Deciding whether unopposed estrogen is the right choice for you may become easier by first determining your risk factors for developing heart disease, or blood clots or having a stroke.

What Are My Risks of Developing Heart Disease, Blood Clots, or Having a Stroke?

Your chances of developing cardiovascular disease after menopause are significantly affected by heredity, diet, and lifestyle. The incidence of cardiovascular disease increases dramatically in women after menopause. Before age fifty, men are six to seven times more likely than women to have heart attacks. After age sixty, a woman's likelihood of suffering a heart attack seems to become about equal with a man's.

Studies indicate that a woman who has early menopause, either naturally or because of surgical removal of her ovaries, is at higher risk of cardiovascular disease.

A woman is at higher risk of developing cardiovascular disease when she has a family history of cardiovascular disease or stroke before the age of fifty-five.

A woman with high blood pressure is more likely to have a stroke. As estrogen levels diminish in a woman's body during and after menopause, it is believed that her LDL creeps upward, her HDL declines, and her risk of developing cardiovascular disease increases. However, there are other factors besides estrogen production that contribute to high cholesterol levels, such as diet and exercise. Elevated cholesterol levels, especially of LDL (bad) cholesterol, can lead to atherosclerosis, the narrowing or blockage of arteries that supply blood to the heart and brain.

Smoking cigarettes is bad for your health altogether, but worse for your cardiovascular system. The more you smoke, the greater your risks. If you have quit smoking, the longer it's been since you stopped, the more your risk decreases.

What Do I Need to Know About Heart Attacks, Blood Clots, and Strokes?

Coronary artery disease is usually caused by atherosclerosis, the narrowing or blockage of arteries that supply blood to the heart and brain, decreasing their supply of oxygen and nutrients. Lack of oxygen and nutrient-rich blood to the heart can lead to heart attack. Lack of oxygen and nutrient-rich blood to the brain can cause stroke.

Narrowing or blockage of the arteries, caused by atherosclerosis, is a result of plaque (cholesterol and other fatty substances) gradually collecting on the inner walls of the arteries. The slow buildup of plaque on artery walls appears to begin early in life, but women are usually protected from blockage of the arteries before menopause because of their natural estrogen production.

A partial blockage of the coronary arteries may result in angina pectoris, severe chest pains that are usually a warning sign that a heart attack could result unless diet adjustments or medical treatment intervene to relieve the blockage. A narrowing of the major arteries supplying blood to the lower body can cause pains in the legs during exercise.

A heart attack occurs when a coronary artery or one of its branches becomes blocked to the point that its supply of blood to the heart stops. That causes the area of the heart not getting blood to die and become scarred.

If a major heart attack occurs, death can result.

Stroke

A stroke is a rupture in a blocked artery supplying blood to the brain. It can result in the loss of various bodily functions, depending on the part of the brain deprived of blood. A woman may lose the strength of grip in her hands; she may lose her balance, becoming unsteady on her feet; or she may lose control of her speech, her words becoming slurred. When a major stroke occurs, sudden death can result.

High blood pressure is a warning sign that you may be at risk of having a stroke; therefore, it is important to monitor your blood pressure, especially after menopause. There are various ways you can reduce your blood pressure:

- HRT may decrease your blood pressure.
- Prescription medication may be needed if you have severe hypertension.
- Dietary changes are extremely effective at reducing high blood pressure and eliminating excess body fat, especially:
  - Reducing fat, sugar, and sodium intake.
  - Increasing daily potassium intake by drinking orange juice and eating raw, fresh vegetables, tomatoes, or apples.

- Using a potassium-based salt substitute such as Morton Salt Substitute, Nu-Salt, or No Salt. However, a woman with kidney problems needs to check with her physician before using these products.
- Taking a calcium, magnesium, and vitamin D supplement to restore mineral balance to the body and relax blood vessels.
- Avoiding crash diets to lose weight as they often deplete the body of vital nutrients.
- Avoiding soft water purified by sodium. Drink bottled water instead.

A woman with extremely high blood pressure or severe diabetes who needs HRT for other reasons may be advised to use the estrogen patch. When estrogen is taken orally, it passes through the liver before entering the general blood circulation. But estrogen through the skin passes through the liver last, causing its effect on the liver to be greatly reduced. The liver converts and stores sugar to be used by the body. It also produces a protein called *renin substrate* that lowers blood pressure. However, when using the patch instead of oral hormones, the benefits of estrogen on blood cholesterol levels are also reduced. Estrogen stimulates production of cholesterol by the liver, usually increasing HDL cholesterol and decreasing LDL.

Cholesterol

Cholesterol is a soft, waxy, fatty substance used by the body to manufacture hormones, bile acid, and vitamin D. It is found in every part of your body, including the nervous system, muscles, skin, liver, intestines, heart, and most other organs.

Cholesterol moves through your body by attaching itself to lipoproteins, two types of proteins that serve different functions.

The two types of lipoproteins measured in your blood are high-density lipoprotein (HDL) and low-density lipoprotein (LDL). LDL delivers cholesterol to where it is needed in the body and deposits it there. HDL takes unneeded cholesterol from the body's cells and tissues and carries it to the liver, where it can be excreted.

The blood contains more LDL than HDL, but levels of both must fall within a normal range for you to have good cardiovascular health.

To determine your cardiovascular health based on blood cholesterol levels, your doctor needs to have your total cholesterol level determined (by means of a blood test), as well as your LDL and HDL levels. The levels of all three are one indication of your cardiovascular health:

- Total cholesterol count lower than 200 is considered good. A count of 200 to 239 borders on high risk, and a count above 239 is considered high risk.
- LDL cholesterol count under 130 is considered good, 130 to 159 borders on high risk, and above 160 is high risk.
- HDL cholesterol count above 55 is considered good, 35 to 55 borders on high risk, and less than 35 is high risk.

If you divide your total cholesterol count by your HDL cholesterol count, a 4.5 or less result is good. Anything above 4.5 indicates a higher risk of cardiovascular disease. It is better for your LDL (bad) cholesterol count to fall into a low range and your HDL (good) cholesterol count to fall into a high range, usually indicating a lower risk for cardiovascular disease.

The body can produce all the cholesterol it needs to function properly, so dietary cholesterol you eat may contribute to higher cholesterol levels if it cannot be carried out of the body effectively. Even though your diet is a strong contributor to your blood cholesterol levels, it is believed there is a genetic predisposition to either healthy or unhealthy cholesterol levels, even with an ideal diet.

A woman with a high total cholesterol level needs to have her HDL and LDL levels checked to see if she is high in the HDL (good) or the LDL (bad).

If your LDL cholesterol count is very high, your doctor may suggest that you take medication to reduce your cholesterol, consider taking estrogen if you are past menopause, lose weight if you are overweight, or consume a low-cholesterol diet.

How Does My Diet and Lifestyle Affect My Cardiovascular Health?

A healthy diet is one limited to no more than 300 mg of cholesterol daily, with less than 30 percent of your calories coming from fat.

The average American diet contains higher than advised levels of cholesterol, with 350 to 450 mg being average, and 35 to 40 percent of caloric intake coming from fat.

A diet high in saturated fats tends to increase cholesterol levels. Saturated fats are found primarily in animal products such as meat and poultry and whole dairy products such as cheese and butter, as well as in coconut and palm oils and any fats that are solid at room temperature.

Instead of saturated fats use unsaturated fats—oils liquid at room temperature, including olive, canola, corn, safflower, soybean, and sunflower. Increase your intake of dietary fiber, which tends to soak up cholesterol, preventing it from being absorbed into your bloodstream, and carry it out of your body.

Foods high in vitamins C, B_6, and E and magnesium are said to lower cholesterol levels, keeping the arteries clean and the blood free flowing. Foods with a natural cholesterol-lowering effect include apples, barley, beans, carrots, chili peppers, eggplant, garlic, grapefruit, lecithin from soybeans, oat bran, onions, plantains (a variety of green banana), seafood, seaweed, soybeans, spinach, yams, and yogurt.

Routine moderate exercise benefits you in many ways, including aiding your cardiovascular health by increasing your circulation and stamina, aiding in weight loss, and reducing stress. The effects of negative stress on the body can be a significant contributor to cardiovascular problems.

The following herbs may be taken on the advice of a health care professional to benefit your individual cardiovascular health needs:

- Ginkgo biloba is used by millions of people in Europe and Asia because of its benefits to the cardiovascular system. It is said to improve circulation and increase the oxygen supply to the heart and other organs, to counteract the effects of angina, and to increase blood supply to the brain, thus improving memory and alertness.
- Hawthorne berries are widely used in Europe to lower cholesterol and as a heart tonic. They are said to strengthen and balance the heart, preventing or reducing irregular heartbeat and protecting against oxygen deficiency.
- Ginseng is said to prevent atherosclerosis and hypertension, and to reduce cholesterol levels.

HRT and Uterine Diseases

Does Taking Hrt Cause Uterine Cancer?

Although uterine cancer was not specifically addressed in news reports of the WHI study of the estrogen/progestin HRT, uterine health is a very real concern for a woman who may be considering whether taking HRT is right for her.

What Do I Need to Know About Hrt and My Urterus?

Estrogen should not be taken without progestins or natural progesterone if your uterus is intact. Continuous stimulation of the uterine lining (endometrium) by the estrogens estradiol and estrone has been shown to increase a woman's chances for developing uterine cancer.

A woman is advised not to take estrogen if she has or has had endometrial cancer.

A woman may be advised not to take estrogen or to take it with extreme caution when she has or has had uterine abnormalities such as endometrial hyperplasia, fibroid tumors (myomas) of the uterus, uterine polyps, endometriosis, or adenomyosis. A woman taking estrogen who develops any of these diseases or conditions is usually advised to stop taking it because these conditions are believed to be estrogen dependent and may become worse when estrogen is taken.

What Should I Look for When Monitoring My Uterine Health?

Postmenopausal bleeding while a woman is taking HRT seriously concerns doctors because it can be a warning sign that the uterine lining (endometrium) is developing abnormalities that could lead to uterine cancer. Always report any bleeding you notice while taking HRT to your physician, and discuss what tests you may need to take to ascertain if the bleeding is caused by uterine abnormalities.

It is important to determine the origin of any abnormal bleeding a woman experiences at any time of her life, but especially after menopause, whether or not she takes HRT.

A pelvic exam will tell the doctor if your uterus feels abnormal or if the bleeding originates in your vagina. If that is not conclusive, a tampon can be useful in determining the source. The tampon is worn for a short period of time. If the bleeding continues and the tampon is free of blood when it is removed, the bleeding most likely comes from the bladder, urethra, or rectum area. A urologic evaluation may be suggested to discover whether the bleeding originates from the bladder, or a proctoscopic exam may be necessary to determine if the bleeding originates in the rectum.

If abnormal bleeding is believed to come from the uterus, various tests may be performed to determine its cause. These tests may be noninvasive, but a surgical procedure may be needed to acquire an endometrial tissue sample for analysis.

A vaginal ultrasound is sometimes used as a precautionary diagnostic evaluation for monitoring the thickness of a woman's uterine lining while she is taking HRT. Generally, if the uterine lining looks normal and the thickness of the endometrium is 5 mm or less, no further tests are warranted. If the endometrium is more than 5 mm thick, further tests are usually advised. Ultrasounds can also diagnose or monitor uterine fibroid tumors.

A medical D and C (dilation and curettage) is hormonal therapy sometimes used if a woman has abnormal uterine bleeding. She takes progesterone pills for seven to fourteen days to cause the uterine lining to shed once the progesterone is stopped, just as it would during a menstrual period. Sometimes this eliminates abnormal uterine bleeding caused by hormonal imbalances; however, an endometrial tissue sample will then be unavailable for analysis that might identify a more serious cause of bleeding. If abnormal bleeding persists after a medical D and C, surgical evaluation may be recommended by the physician.

What Surgical Procedures May Be Needed to Determine the Cause of Uterine Bleeding?

Various surgical procedures are used to determine the cause of abnormal uterine bleeding, including:

- An endometrial biopsy, where a thin tube is inserted through the cervix into the uterus. An instrument scrapes the uterine lining and traps samples of tissue that are withdrawn along with the tube. This endometrial tissue sample is evaluated by a laboratory.
- Aspiration of the uterine cavity, which is performed by inserting a thin tube through the cervix into the uterus. A syringe or suction machine attached to the tube suctions the uterine lining, removing more tissue than is taken for an endometrial biopsy. This tissue sample is also evaluated by a laboratory.
- Surgical D and C, which is performed by dilating the cervical opening, then inserting a spoon-shaped instrument into the uterus to scrape and remove as much of the uterine lining as necessary. These tissue samples are evaluated by a laboratory.
- Hysteroscopy, which is performed by inserting a narrow light-containing telescope through the cervix into the uterus so the

physician can look inside the uterus for abnormalities. A biopsy, aspiration, or D and C may then be performed if needed.

What Types of Uterine Abnormalities Might Be Found During These Kinds of Tests?

These tests are usually performed to determine the cause of abnormal uterine bleeding, which may include endometrial hyperplasia, endometrial cancer, uterine polyps, endometriosis, adenomyosis, or fibroid tumors.

Fibroid Tumors

A uterine fibroid (myoma or leiomyoma) is a benign growth of the uterine muscle that may be as small as a pea or as large as a basketball. About one out of every four women over age thirty has uterine fibroids, with African American women having them more frequently.

Smaller fibroids are usually painless and symptomless. Larger fibroids often can be felt through the abdominal cavity and may cause pain, pressure, and a feeling of heaviness in the abdomen. They may cause excessive uterine bleeding, constipation because of pressure on the rectum, and frequent urination due to pressure on the bladder.

Your doctor may suspect you have a uterine fibroid if your uterus feels hard, lumpy, enlarged, or irregularly shaped. Ultrasound may be recommended to confirm a uterine fibroid, as opposed to a more serious pelvic condition.

Uterine fibroids are benign and do not turn into cancer. They are usually not treated unless they grow large enough to cause pain or excessive menstrual bleeding. Because they are believed to be caused by excessive estrogen stimulation of the uterus, a woman with a uterine fibroid is usually advised not to take estrogen during and after menopause. Uterine fibroids often atrophy after menopause when a woman's natural production of estrogen drops off.

Some women with uterine fibroids may decide to take HRT for other health reasons (the benefits to their cardiovascular system or bones) but are extra cautious about the types and dosages of hormones they take. Careful monitoring is then needed.

Uterine Polyps

A uterine polyp is a growth that forms in the lining of the uterus, called an endometrial polyp, or in the endocervix, the canal leading to the uterine cavity. Polyps form for various reasons, including excessive estrogen stimulation, and commonly occur during menopausal years when a woman's hormone production becomes erratic. They may also develop from a small piece of pregnancy tissue left behind after childbirth, abortion, or miscarriage. There appears to be a hereditary tendency to develop polyps.

Uterine polyps are usually benign, especially during a woman's thirties and forties, but the chances of their being malignant (cancerous) increase somewhat after menopause. Endocervical polyps that develop before or after menopause are almost always benign.

Either abnormal menstrual bleeding and spotting or very heavy and prolonged periods can be a symptom of polyps. Your physician may be able to see endocervical polyps protruding from your cervix during a pelvic exam, but uterine polyps hide within uterine tissue and can be confirmed only by a more extensive endometrial examination, such as a D and C or a hysteroscopy.

Endometriosis

Endometriosis is a disease caused by the uterine glands and tissue migrating outside the uterine cavity and invading other pelvic areas.

Endometriosis can cause severe menstrual cramps, painful periods, and ovarian cysts, and can interfere with ovarian function. Endometriosis usually disappears after menopause when estrogen production by the ovaries diminishes.

Adenomyosis, also called internal endometriosis, occurs when the glands inside the uterine cavity grow into the muscle of the uterus. Commonly found during the menopausal years when hormone production is imbalanced by excessive estrogen, adenomyosis may cause heavy bleeding and prolonged menstrual periods, with a feeling of heaviness in the abdomen. During a pelvic exam, a woman's doctor may find her uterus enlarged, soft, and tender but smooth (unlike when fibroids are present, which cause the uterus to feel hard and lumpy).

Endometrial Hyperplasia

Endometrial hyperplasia occurs when the glands and tissue of the uterine lining multiply, resulting in an abnormal number of glands that appear to be lying on top of each other rather than separated by supporting tissue. In severe cases (atypical endometrial hyperplasia), cells within the glands become irregular. Although this is usually benign cell development, it may be a warning sign that the development of endometrial cancer is possible.

Endometrial tissue samples will need to be taken and analyzed to determine if they are normal or appear to have the abnormal development associated with cancer.

In endometrial cancer, the glands invade the supporting tissue around the uterus. If that invasion progresses, it can spread to other vital organs.

The most common sign of endometrial hyperplasia or endometrial cancer is abnormal uterine bleeding, which is why it is important to report any abnormal bleeding to your physician, especially when you take estrogen.

Does Taking Estrogen Cause Endometrial Hyperplasia or Endomentrial Cancer?

Cancer is not caused by taking estrogen, but excessive estrogen stimulation of the endometrial lining without progesterone to balance it can result in endometrial hyperplasia and can lead to endometrial cancer.

Anything that causes the uterus to receive excessive estrogen stimulation without progesterone to counteract the uterine lining building up makes a woman more prone to develop these diseases. That would include women who take estrogen during and after menopause without a progestin or natural progesterone.

Before menopause, a woman who does not ovulate regularly, especially if she has only a few menstrual periods a year, is at higher risk for developing endometrial hyperplasia or endometrial cancer. A woman who is very overweight is also at higher risk because her body fat converts androgens to estrogen.

Conclusion

Determining whether HRT is too risky for you to consider requires an assessment of your breast cancer, cardiovascular disease, and uterine cancer risks; an evaluation by a doctor of your medical records and medical history; a thorough physical examination; and laboratory testing. Only then can your current overall health status and potential health risks be evaluated realistically.

Statistics released in July 2002 by the Women's Health Initiative (WHI) of the National Institutes of Health, based on their most recent study of estrogen/progestin combination HRT, revealed that participants' breast cancer risks increased while taking the HRT, as did their heart disease risks. For these reasons the study was abruptly stopped three years earlier than was planned.

The WHI is conducting a companion study, which is ongoing, to determine what the risks might be of taking estrogen alone for women who have had hysterectomies. Although information has not been released from that study, it is continuing uninterrupted.

Making the hormone decision when considering the high-risk factors of breast cancer and heart disease may not be easy. A multitude of studies have been conducted using various hormones and hormone combinations. Although results of those studies may, at times, appear to be inconsistent, most actually reach the same conclusions:

- A woman with high-risk factors for breast cancer should very carefully consider whether taking HRT that includes estrogen will benefit her.
- A woman with high-risk factors for heart disease, blood clots, and stroke should very carefully consider whether HRT that includes estrogen and progestin will benefit her. After a

hysterectomy, estrogen alone may be safer, unless your breast cancer risk is high.

- A woman with a history of uterine disorders associated with estrogen sensitivity should very carefully consider whether taking HRT that includes estrogen will benefit her. Estrogen without progestin should not be taken by a woman with an intact uterus.
- Routine monitoring of your health is very important when taking HRT.

Question 5

If I Start on HRT, Do I Have to Keep Taking It After Menopause?

Many women decide to take HRT to relieve physical and emotional discomforts or distress they experience during the menopausal transition, putting off the decision about continuing to take HRT until after their menopause has concluded. This is understandable when the risks associated with taking HRT are so overwhelming.

If you are taking HRT during your menopausal transition, you have time to think about whether you want to continue. It's your choice. If you haven't chosen to take HRT for menopausal discomforts, you still have time to consider whether HRT can benefit you after your menopause is complete.

Most of the information you need to know about HRT and your body has already been presented in this book. The rest can be found in these last three chapters. The effects of long-term use of HRT on your bones, your pelvic organs, and your appearance are included in this chapter.

One piece of information about your bones is very important: During the first three to ten years after menopause, your bones lose more mass than they will during any comparable period of time in the rest of your life. Now is the time to start deciding how you are going to give your bones the support they need to carry you through the rest of your life.

If you're approaching the menopausal age or are already going through menopause, you may already be seeing how your lifestyle choices affect your health and vitality. When it comes to the health of your bones, this is especially true. Making healthy lifestyle choices and making informed health care choices are both important; one affects the other.

How Can I Keep My Bones Healthy After Menopause?

You've considered all the risks factors associated with taking HRT, and you know that breast cancer, heart disease, and uterine cancer risk factors probably seem like the most important, but now you've got to think about your bones.

For many women the risk of developing osteoporosis may be the most important factor to consider when deciding whether to take HRT after menopause. If you already know you can't take HRT, or you choose not to, there are lots of lifestyle changes you can make to enhance your bone health. Whether or not you're taking HRT to ease yourself through the menopausal transition, the next several years are crucial for your future bone health.

How Does HRT Affect My Bones?

Studies have shown that taking HRT is beneficial for the bones of most women, especially when combined with adequate nutritional intake and appropriate exercise.

At one time estrogen alone was prescribed for menopausal and postmenopausal women because it alleviated the discomforts of menopause and slowed bone loss. This appeared to result in good bone density, but a woman's bones become more brittle as she gets older because her bone tissue ages as she does. Knowing that progesterone stimulates the formation of healthy new bone, the medical community began to prescribe progestins along with estrogen. This combination contributed to the formation of new bone to some degree but did not appear to effectively reproduce natural bone remodeling.

Studies indicate that a treatment program of natural progesterone with estrogen, when needed, may be an even more effective treatment for osteoporosis in postmenopausal women. Natural progesterone, which is molecularly identical to the progesterone produced by a woman's ovaries, has been shown to stimulate healthy new bone formation, especially when combined with adequate nutrition and exercise.

If you decide to take HRT to prevent or treat osteoporosis, it is often recommended that it be continued for the rest of your life. Usually, taking HRT for bone protection begins at the end of menopause because bone loss seems to be most dramatic during the first three to ten years after the ovaries stop producing hormones. After that, the degree of bone loss tapers off dramatically but continues to decline gradually for the rest of a woman's life.

If I Completed Menopause Over Three Years Ago, Is It Too Late for HRT?

The experts agree that it's never too late to begin HRT. However, those who advocate HRT consisting of estrogen with progestins will tell you that further bone loss can be avoided, but new bone formation is not a realistic expectation. On the other hand, doctors advocating the use of natural progesterone with estrogen have seen the formation of healthy new bone in their patients.

The success of either HRT program requires lifestyle adjustments that include adequate nutrition, appropriate weight-bearing exercise, and the elimination of destructive lifestyle habits.

If I Stop HRT, Will the Benefits Stay with Me?

The benefits of taking HRT usually stop when the treatment does. Some doctors say even if you do decide to stop taking HRT at some point beyond the three-to-ten-year period of greatest bone loss, you're better off because you've maintained more bone mass than you would have otherwise. Others say that when you stop taking HRT your body adjusts as though you just completed menopause, with the escalated bone loss occurring.

Many women who don't want to take or stay on conventional HRT choose to take instead a more natural combination estrogen called tri-estrogen. It contains 80 percent estriol with 10 percent estrone and 10 percent estradiol. When taken in a dosage of 2.5 mg for twenty-five-day cycles with natural progesterone added at 25 to 50 mg during the last two weeks of the cycle, it is said to effectively relieve the discomforts of menopause and protect against bone deterioration, without having a negative effect on breast tissue.

It must be stressed that the use of estriol and natural progesterone has not undergone the scientific blind studies commonly recognized as proof of effectiveness by the American medical community.

How Do I Know If I Need HRT for Healthy Bones?

The most common risk factors are as follows:

- Are you Caucasian or Asian, with a small, thin body type?
- Is there a history of osteoporosis or hip fractures in your family?
- Have you completed menopause either naturally or due to a hysterectomy?
- Has it been necessary for you to take thyroid medication or cortisone-like drugs for asthma or arthritis for a long period of time, or cancer treatment?
- Do you smoke cigarettes or drink alcoholic beverages in more than moderate amounts?

The best way to determine if you are developing osteoporosis or if you have significant bone loss is with a bone scan, which measures your bone density. If you have not had a bone scan before menopause to establish a bone density baseline, then your test results will be compared to the average woman. Therefore, women who fall into a high-risk category for osteoporosis may choose to have a baseline bone scan earlier in life to determine what is normal for them.

What Can I Do to Prevent Osteoporosis?

Your bones are especially sensitive to the hormonal changes that take place during and after menopause. HRT can help you maintain good bone health, especially when combined with adequate nutrition and appropriate lifestyle choices.

The basic lifestyle factors that you can control to diminish the development of osteoporosis include:

- Make dietary changes that provide adequate nutritional support to your body.
- Eliminate destructive dietary choices by avoiding excessive sugar consumption, excessive caffeine consumption by drinking coffee and tea and eating chocolate, excessive hard liquor consumption, and excessive consumption of red meat and processed and refined foods.
- Develop and maintain an appropriate weight-bearing exercise routine.
- Reduce the destructive effects of stress and anxiety on the body.
- Stop smoking cigarettes.
- Avoid exposure to environmental toxins and heavy metals such as lead, chlorine, and fluoride in drinking water, and aluminum in antiperspirants, medications, and cookware.
- Avoid as much as possible the long-term use of thyroid, arthritis, or asthma medications, antibiotics, diuretics, and laxatives.
- Get professional help to overcome eating disorders such as bulimia, anorexia nervosa, or a serious loss of appetite resulting in low caloric intake and malabsorption of nutrients by the body.

Dietary Choices

All factors considered, the importance of good food choices cannot be overemphasized as a first step toward healthy bones. Adequate nutrition from a healthy diet builds bones throughout your life, helps your bones stay strong as you get older, and contributes to the overall good health of your body and mind.

Poor food choices and consumption can block bone-building, cause your bones to deteriorate faster, and adversely affect your physical health and emotional well-being.

A well-balanced diet of fresh, unprocessed foods in the form of whole grains, vegetables, and fruits is best. Some studies show that vegetarians who follow a low-fat, non–junk food diet have healthier bones when they enter menopause, and they lose bone at a slower rate after menopause.

Foods that contribute to good bone health include those with plenty of calcium, magnesium, and potassium, such as broccoli, leafy green vegetables, sprouts, carrots, sea vegetables such as kelp, fish and seafood, eggs, yogurt, kefir, bananas, apples, cranberries, apricots, dried fruits, nuts and seeds, beans, soy products such as tofu and miso, and molasses. Alfalfa has a very high calcium content and is the food eaten by most dairy cows. Also, apple cider vinegar can be used as a salad dressing on fresh vegetables to help the body absorb calcium by raising the pH (alkalinity) of the body.

Specific dietary tips for healthy bones include:

- Reduce your use of salt. It appears that high sodium intake may result in excess calcium excretion in the urine. Some individuals are hypersensitive to salt, and the effect is dramatically magnified with even moderate salt intake.
- Consume dairy products in moderation. Dairy products are a good source of calcium; however, they also have drawbacks. The fat content of the most calcium-rich dairy products could be a problem for women who need to be on a low-fat

diet. The butterfat in dairy products helps the body absorb calcium and other nutrients, so whole milk or cheese products are a better source of calcium than nonfat or low-fat dairy products. Also, pasteurized milk is sometimes difficult for women to digest as they get older. Some experts claim synthetic vitamin D added to milk can deplete the body of magnesium.

Cultured dairy products, especially yogurt with active cultures, may be the best choice for dairy intake because they are more easily digested and the beneficial bacteria promote absorption of nutrients through the intestines.

Ice cream is a good source of calcium; however, most ice cream is loaded with sugar, which has no nutritional value, and it is generally agreed that refined sugar is detrimental to the health of most people.

- Avoid red meats and reduce animal protein and fat consumption. Meat contains twenty-five times more phosphorus than calcium; therefore, excessive meat consumption disturbs the healthy calcium/phosphorus balance of the body (twice as much calcium as phosphorus). Studies have shown that the urinary excretion of calcium increases when animal protein and fats are consumed.
- Avoid eating refined flours, processed foods, and junk foods. Refined flours and processed foods contain a low nutritional intake for the amount of food that is eaten. Their consumption provides empty calories to a woman's body during and after menopause when nutritional intake is very important for maintaining good bone health.
- As much as possible, eliminate from your diet sugar, caffeine, and soft drinks.

Sugar. It is well known that refined sugar is not nutritious and is high in calories. Studies have shown that sugar intake results in a measured increase in calcium excreted in the urine, suggesting that sugar depletes the body of calcium. If over 90 percent of your body's calcium is in your bones, sugar consumption is likely to leach calcium from the bones, thus reducing their calcium content.

Caffeine. Other studies indicate that caffeine causes calcium to be lost from the body. The higher your caffeine consumption, the greater the calcium loss. Restricting your caffeine consumption is known to benefit your bone health. Moreover, all coffee, even decaffeinated, disturbs the pH balance of your body, making it more acidic. After you drink coffee, your body tries to rebalance its pH by drawing calcium from your bones.

Soft drinks. Caffeine-free soft drinks may still be loaded with sugar or artificial sweeteners, which are both bad for the body. But even worse than that, soft drinks are high in phosphorus. The calcium/phosphorus balance of the body, with twice as much calcium as phosphorus, is very important for good bone health. Excessive phosphorus intake throws off that balance and causes calcium to be excreted in the urine.

Excessive alcoholic beverages. It is well documented that there is a high incidence of osteoporosis in male alcoholics because alcohol affects the liver's metabolism of calcium and vitamin D. Although similar studies have not been conducted with groups of women, it is assumed that the conclusions would be the same.

Moderate consumption of alcohol is a subject of some debate. Some studies suggest that moderate daily alcohol intake is beneficial to otherwise healthy individuals. Other studies conclude that any alcohol consumption is not good for the body. Everyone agrees that excessive consumption of alcohol is toxic to the body.

How Much Calcium Intake Is Needed for Healthy Bones?

The recommended daily allowance (RDA) of calcium for the average adult is 1,000 mg. However, it is suggested that women increase their daily intake of calcium to 1,500 mg during and after menopause.

Are Specific Vitamins and Minerals Better for My Bones?

Various vitamins and minerals interact within the body for proper metabolism and assimilation of all the nutrients you ingest, but the following nutrients are particularly important for good bone health:

- Vitamin D is needed so the body can properly absorb calcium. Vitamin D is manufactured within the body as a result of exposure to sunlight. It can be obtained by eating eggs, some fish, and butter, or by taking cod liver oil.
- Magnesium is important so the body can use vitamin D and retain calcium. It can be obtained by eating leafy green vegetables, whole grains, nuts and seeds, beans, and eggs. High phosphorus intake causes the body to become magnesium deficient. Soft drinks are very high in phosphorus.
- Boron helps the body retain calcium and magnesium. It can be obtained by eating leafy green vegetables, especially alfalfa, kelp, spinach, lettuce, and cabbage, and from apples and beans.
- Silicon is important for formation of the soft tissue in bone that keeps bones flexible. Silicon can be obtained by eating grains with fiber, especially brown rice, oats, and barley, as well as many fruits and vegetables. The herbs horsetail and hemp nettle are also good sources of silicon.

- Vitamin C contributes to collagen formation in bones. Vitamin C can be obtained by eating leafy green vegetables, cauliflower, tomatoes, fruits, and berries. Smoking depletes the body of vitamin C.
- Hydrochloric acid (HCl) is important for the body to absorb calcium. HCl is naturally produced by the stomach, but production appears to diminish as we get older. Stress, anxiety, and antacids all reduce HCl production in the stomach.

Can I Get Enough Vitamins and Minerals from Food or Are Supplements Needed?

Unfortunately, even under ideal circumstances, most women in the United States have difficulty consuming and assimilating enough nutrients from food alone. Therefore, preventing and treating osteoporosis usually requires more than a good diet, although adequate nutrition is very important because it provides balanced nutrients to the body.

However, without consistent, conscientious effort, it is usually difficult to get enough calcium and other nutrients from food during and after menopause when the nutritional requirements of your body increase. The dietary calcium intake of the average woman is estimated to be about 400 to 500 mg a day. Therefore, a daily calcium supplement of 500 to 1,000 mg is suggested for most women over age thirty-five.

A good multiple vitamin/mineral supplement is recommended for most menopausal and postmenopausal women for maintaining optimal overall health, especially the health of their bones.

Selecting a nutritional supplement can be confusing because there are so many available, with varying combinations and quantities of nutrients. Since every person's genetic makeup, diet, and lifestyle differ, each individual must assess her own supplemental needs. Consulting with a nutritionist may be advisable, or numerous books that address diet and nutrition may be helpful.

The following basic guidelines for daily supplemental intake have been shown to contribute to good bone health and fall within the safe ranges for most women. Do not exceed safe levels without the advice of a health care professional you trust. It may be beneficial for you to discuss this list with your physician or to seek the assistance of a health care professional with nutritional training.

Minerals: calcium, 500 to 1,200 mg; magnesium, 250 to 600 mg; zinc, 10 to 30 mg; manganese, 5 to 20 mg; boron, 1 to 3 mg; silicon, 1 to 2 mg; copper, 1 to 2 mg; strontium, 0.5 to 3 mg

Vitamins: vitamin C, 100 to 1,000 mg; vitamin D, 100 to 400 IU; vitamin B_6, 5 to 50 mg; folic acid, 0.5 to 5 mg; vitamin K, 100 to 500 mcg

Supplements are best utilized by the body when they are ingested as food would be, in small amounts a few times a day, rather than all at one time. It is better to take most supplements with food, but others are best taken between meals. There are usually instructions on the containers if this is important.

Often mineral supplements are best taken at night or between meals; it may be difficult for the body to absorb calcium in particular when it is ingested with any of the following: excessive dietary fiber or cooked cereals and grains; spinach, squash, rhubarb, parsley, beets, and beans; caffeine in coffee, tea, sodas, and chocolate; and antacids.

Some nutritional supplements can alter the effects of prescription medications within the body. You need to ask your physician if the quantities of nutritional supplements you plan to take are safe with your prescription medications.

Because herbs are derived from plants, they do have nutritional value. As with all nutritional supplements, caution is needed when taking herbs. Many herbs are potent and can have a strong effect on your body. It is best to take herbs in small quantities and with the advice of a health care professional with a knowledge of herbs.

Some mineral/vitamin formulations also contain herbs, and health food stores carry herbal combinations specifically formulated for good bone health. The following herbs may be included:

- Black walnut contains silica.
- Comfrey contains calcium and phosphorus.
- Horsetail and rue strengthen bones.
- Oat straw is high in silica and calcium.
- Queen of the meadow contains vitamin D.
- Skullcap contains calcium and magnesium.
- White oak bark and marshmallow contain calcium.

Are Tums a Good Source of Calcium?

Tums has been suggested as a good source of calcium; however, there is some controversy about this. While a Tums tablet does contain 200 mg of calcium carbonate, its purpose is to reduce stomach acid (HCl), which slows down digestion, and is said to reduce calcium absorption by the body.

Tums do not contain aluminum. Avoid antacids that contain aluminum, which is detrimental to a woman's bone health. (Aluminum leaches calcium from the body, disturbing your calcium balance. Besides avoiding antacids containing aluminum, avoid cooking in aluminum containers, especially highly acidic foods such as tomatoes and tomato sauces. It's also recommended that you eliminate antiperspirants containing aluminum.)

What Type of Exercise Is Best for My Bones?

Weight-bearing exercise benefits your bones and muscles as well as provides the overall health benefits derived from regular moderate exercise. Strong muscles provide better support for your bones. Studies have shown that moderate weight-bearing exercise causes bones to become stronger. People who are right-handed and use that hand more often usually have slightly larger bones in their right hands and arms. Astronauts who have lived in a weightless environment for extended periods of time have been shown to experience bone loss.

Bicycling and swimming are not weight-bearing exercises that build and strengthen bones, although they may be beneficial for the body in other ways. It is best to avoid excessive aerobic exercise that may lead to low body fat, which has an effect on hormonal balances in the body and is not beneficial for your bones. Many women athletes, such as marathon runners, ballerinas, and gymnasts, stop menstruating altogether even before they reach menopausal age due to low body fat.

Any routine, moderate weight-bearing exercise is beneficial. Although there's no "best" activity, walking may be the easiest form of exercise for most people. Walking outdoors for one hour, two to three times a week is beneficial not only for your bones, but also for your heart and your emotional well-being. Outdoor exercise during the day has an added benefit because the body manufactures vitamin D in response to sunlight exposure.

What Other Factors Could Affect My Bone Health?

Exposure to heavy metals and environmental toxins may increase your risk of osteoporosis by leaching calcium and vitamin D from your body. Avoid:

- Exposure to aluminum in antiperspirants, antacids, cookware, some baking powder, food and beverage containers, children's aspirin, and air conditioning
- Exposure to tin in cans used for food packaging
- Cadmium in cigarette smoke
- Fluoride, chlorine, and other toxins in drinking water
- Electric blankets, nonfiltered computer screens, and fluorescent lights

There is evidence that your risk of developing osteoporosis may increase if you take prescription medications, especially the following:

- Glucocorticosteroids such as cortisone and prednisone over an extended period of time interfere with bone remodeling, absorption of calcium, and retention of potassium.
- Thyroid medication over an extended period of time may increase your risk for developing osteoporosis. Although

there is contradictory information coming from studies of women taking thyroid medication, it is a fact that interaction of the thyroid with the other glands of the body is important for bone remodeling. Medications that affect the thyroid functions within the body will also affect the bones.

- Antibiotics taken on a regular basis destroy beneficial bacteria in the intestines that are needed for adequate absorption of nutrients. After taking antibiotics, you can reestablish beneficial bacteria in the body by eating yogurt with active cultures or by taking acidophilus supplements available at health food stores.
- Laxatives and diuretics taken on a regular basis interfere with calcium absorption and may deplete the body of other essential minerals such as magnesium and potassium.

Estrogen replacement is also prescription medication and deserves the same attention to side effects and precautions as any other medical treatment program. Some studies have shown that taking estrogen without added progesterone does reduce bone loss, but your bones may become more brittle.

Any medication could put you at higher risk for developing osteoporosis. Discuss with your physician the side effects of over-the-counter medications as well as necessary prescription medications, and the medications' interaction with your diet and nutritional supplements, as well as a regular exercise program.

How Does HRT Affect My Pelvic Organs?

Taking estrogen after menopause can have a beneficial effect on the condition of your vagina, bladder, and urinary tract but can be detrimental to your uterine lining (as discussed in Chapter 4). Progestins or natural progesterone have a protective effect on the lining of the uterus. A woman with an intact uterus is usually advised to take a progestin or natural progesterone along with estrogen as HRT.

Pelvic Organs: The Vagina

Because vaginal atrophy is directly related to the body's production of estrogen, taking estrogen after menopause has been shown to significantly decrease a woman's chances of developing vaginal atrophy. Some foods, supplements, and herbs also have an estrogenic effect on the body, and those discussed in Chapter 7 may be useful for keeping your pelvic organs toned by maintaining tissue elasticity during and after menopause.

Taking estrogen also eliminates postmenopausal vaginitis some women experience after menopause. Women who have recurring vaginitis after menopause and need to take antibiotics to treat vaginal inflammation and infection caused by lack of estrogen may be advised to consider taking estrogen to reestablish vaginal mucus and increase the thickness of their vaginal tissue.

Estrogen cream inserted vaginally has been shown to be very helpful in treating vaginal atrophy and vaginitis. It improves lubrication and enhances the thickness of vaginal tissue when used a few times a week. However, estrogen applied vaginally still gets absorbed into a woman's general circulation, and the rate of absorption is not as predictable as other types of estrogen intake.

A woman who cannot take estrogen orally needs to discuss with her physician whether it is safe for her to insert small amounts of estrogen cream vaginally to prevent vaginal atrophy or vaginitis.

All health factors need to be considered and close monitoring may be needed, especially if irregular bleeding or other symptoms occur in conjunction with estrogen cream use.

Besides HRT, What Might Help My Pelvic Organs After Menopause?

Regular sexual intercourse is said to help keep a woman's vagina from becoming shorter as her estrogen levels start dropping. A woman who is not sexually active can dilate her vagina with her fingers a few times a week, using a water-soluble lubricant to avoid irritation to the thinning vaginal tissue. Medical supply companies sell vaginal dilators for women who are not comfortable using their fingers.

Vaginal lubricants effectively eliminate vaginal dryness, reduce vaginal irritation during intercourse, and reduce the incidence of vaginitis. Water-soluble lubricants are best. Avoid lubricants that contain perfumes or chemicals, as well as petroleum-based lubricants (such as petroleum jelly and mineral oils), because they may irritate the delicate vaginal lining and increase your risk of developing vaginitis.

Vitamin E vaginal suppositories or a few drops of vitamin E liquid inserted into the vagina a few times a week have also been shown to be an effective alternative to estrogen.

An alternative to antibiotics, folk remedies have been used for centuries in treating yeastlike inflammations and irritations of the vagina. They include yogurt (with active culture) douches, eating yogurt or garlic, and taking acidophilus capsules daily, while avoiding sugar, including very sweet fruit.

If you have to take antibiotics, they will destroy the beneficial bacteria in the body, and recurrence of the condition may result, as well as possible urinary tract or bladder irritation or infection. You can reestablish your body's beneficial bacteria by eating yogurt with active cultures or by taking acidophilus.

Practical tips for avoiding and arresting vaginal irritation include avoiding tight-fitting clothing that does not allow for air circulation in the vaginal area, avoiding panties and pantyhose with dyes that may be irritating, and avoiding laundry detergents and fabric softeners that can irritate delicate vaginal tissue.

Pelvic Organs: The Bladder and Urinary Tract

Taking estrogen can reduce the problem of urinary incontinence and atrophy of the bladder in postmenopausal women. Estrogen improves the capillary blood flow and nerve supply to the pelvic organs, helps tone and improve the elasticity of the tissues supporting the bladder, and thickens urethral tissue, improving a woman's ability to control the urine loss that leads to urinary incontinence.

Estrogen also can strongly contribute to a woman's maintaining her bladder control well into the later years. However, eventually natural aging will result in some loss of nerve supply to the bladder. A woman in her eighties may experience some loss of bladder control even if she is taking estrogen. In extreme cases of urinary incontinence or loss of bladder control, surgery may be needed.

Besides HRT, What Can I Do for My Bladder and Urinary Tract?

Bladder infections often start in the urethra, then spread to the bladder. Antibiotics taken for bladder infections can destroy the body's friendly bacteria and may lead to recurrent bladder infections, as well as to vaginal irritation and infection. Reestablishing beneficial bacteria in the body by taking acidophilus or eating yogurt with active cultures has been shown to be helpful.

Folk remedies to alleviate bladder infection include eating fresh cranberries or garlic and drinking cranberry juice, cherry juice, or corn silk tea.

Taking vitamin C has also been shown to be helpful in soothing and healing inflammations that cause urinary and genital ailments.

How Can Long-term HRT Affect My Appearance?

Taking HRT during and after menopause has been shown to affect a woman's body shape, hair, and skin both positively and negatively, depending on the woman and the types and dosages of the hormones she is taking. HRT appears to delay the effects of aging for a time but does not stop the natural aging process, which can be strongly influenced by a woman's genetic factors, as well as her diet and lifestyle.

Estrogen has been shown to have a beneficial effect on a woman's skin and breasts by causing them to seem fuller, with less sagging. However, this plumping-up effect that pleases some women causes others to complain that taking estrogen results in fluid retention, a bloated feeling, and weight gain. Some women have experienced hair loss while taking estrogen.

My Appearance: Body Weight and Shape

Because progestins affect the uterus, women taking them along with estrogen have complained of abdominal bloating and fluid retention.

Natural progesterone is identical in molecular structure to the progesterone produced by the body, as compared to molecularly altered progestins. Therefore, natural progesterone does not produce the same negative effects on the body as progestins. It has been reported that natural progesterone reduces fluid retention and has an antiwrinkling effect on the skin.

Changes in the breasts are also quite common, including breasts that feel more tender and fuller. Breast changes while taking HRT are potentially serious and are addressed in Chapter 4.

Changes in your body weight or metabolism may result from imbalanced thyroid function. Medications are prescribed for cases of extreme thyroid malfunction. However, these must be taken with caution because thyroid medications can increase a woman's risk of osteoporosis. One in four women in the United States takes medication for thyroid malfunction.

Less extreme thyroid malfunction may be influenced by dietary adjustments and nutritional supplements.

Low thyroid function can be caused by lack of iodine, zinc, and copper in the diet. These can be supplied to the body by eating kelp or seaweed, cantaloupe, fish, beans, chard or turnip greens, peanuts, soy foods, or sunflower seeds, or by taking cod liver oil supplements derived from sea vegetables such as kelp and dulse. Iodine supplements should be taken in extremely limited amounts so as not to throw the thyroid imbalance off to the other extreme. It is best to discuss this issue with a health care professional before trying supplements.

Foods that suppress thyroid function include cabbage, rutabagas, and turnips. Certain drugs and chemicals can also suppress thyroid function, including estrogen (especially the high doses taken in birth control pills), antidiabetic drugs, and sulfa drugs, as well as thyocyanide, a chemical found in cigarette smoke, and fluoride in tap water.

An overactive thyroid depletes the body of calcium, essential fatty acids, and vitamins B_1 and B_6 (take a B-complex supplement and extra B_1 and B_6). High thyroid function can also benefit from foods or supplements containing vitamins C, D, and E.

Appearance: My Skin

Estrogen makes the skin feel fuller and more resilient because it encourages skin cells to take up more water. It causes fat to be distributed within the deep skin layers, giving it support and firmness. Estrogen aids collagen protein production within the skin, helping it maintain a healthy thickness.

It has been reported that taking estrogen will stop the development of wrinkles to some degree, as well as minimize existing wrinkles to some extent. However, nothing is known to stop the natural aging process entirely. Because of the potential serious side effects of HRT, most doctors will not prescribe HRT for a woman who does not otherwise need it, simply because it may delay skin wrinkling for a time.

Women with more body fat appear to maintain less wrinkled skin longer than thin women. Heavier women usually have more estrogen stored in body fat, their body fat supports the outer layer of the skin, and they usually have more fluid content in their skin.

How Long Does It Take for the Beneficial Effects of HRT to Show Up In My Skin?

If your skin has already started to change because of diminished hormone production and you begin taking estrogen, it will probably take several months before you will see an improvement in your skin.

Whether or not you choose to take HRT for health reasons after menopause, there are some general guidelines you can follow to maintain healthy-looking skin:

- Drink at least six to eight glasses of fresh, toxin-free water every day to keep your skin hydrated from the inside. Avoid fluoridated water. Fluoride contributes to skin wrinkling and weakens bones, ligaments, muscles, and tendons, speeding up the aging process.
- Supply moisture to your skin from the outside as well. Use a good moisturizer on your skin at all times and avoid soaps that cause your skin to become dry. A humidifier can help keep your environment moister if you live in a dry climate or if you heat your home during cold months.
- Avoid excessive exposure to skin-damaging sun. Protect your skin with sunscreen during outdoor activity.
- Exercise regularly to improve blood circulation to your skin while toning your muscles.
- Avoid rapid weight loss if you are overweight and want to reduce. A slower weight-loss program will allow your skin to adjust instead of wrinkle, shrinking along with any fat and fluid supporting it.

A healthy diet featuring fresh, unprocessed foods is a good beginning. Specific vitamins and minerals that have been shown to benefit the skin include:

- Vitamin A and beta-carotene (the antioxidants), vitamin E, and the mineral selenium
- Vitamin C, which promotes collagen production
- Vitamin F (essential fatty acids—EFAs), which supports the fatty layer of the skin and protects against skin dehydration

Your health care professional may also suggest you take herbs to enhance your overall health and also benefit your skin during menopause. An herb that is especially helpful for skin is horsetail, sometimes called shave grass (*Equisetum arvense*). It contains silica, a component of collagen in the skin, hair, nails, bones, and teeth. It is said that horsetail enhances youthfulness of the body.

Increased perspiration may occur during menopause if there is not enough estrogen present to balance the androgens. Androgens, male hormones produced by a woman's adrenal glands and ovaries, stimulate sweat glands in the deep skin layer. Often HRT can eliminate the excessive perspiration some women experience during menopause.

Appearance: My Hair

Some women complain that they experience hair thinning and loss after starting to take HRT. This may be because HRT can deplete the body of vitamin B_6, a critical nutrient for healthy hair growth.

Generally, HRT has been shown to counteract hair loss by resupplying nourishment and support to the hair follicles. It usually prevents unwanted androgen-stimulated hair growth as well.

There is no evidence that hair graying is related to menopause and taking HRT is not known to reverse graying hair to its original color.

Once a woman starts taking HRT, it will usually take several months before she will see its effects on her hair.

Adequate nutritional intake is beneficial for your hair, as is limiting saturated fats, refined foods, sugars, alcohol, and caffeine. Specific foods that are good for your hair include apples, bananas, carrots, cucumbers, eggs, green peppers, leafy green vegetables, onions, and strawberries. Vitamins and minerals that are beneficial for the skin will also benefit the hair, as will the herb horsetail.

Conclusion

Osteoporosis is a serious disease that can be debilitating, causing pain and bones that break or fracture easily. During the first three to ten years after menopause concludes a woman loses more bone mass that she will during any comparable period of time in the rest of her life. Therefore, it is prudent to begin making decisions about how you will provide the support your body needs to maintain healthy bones before your menopause concludes. Deciding on HRT or choosing to live a bone-healthy lifestyle may depend on your osteoporosis risk factors, as well as your risk factors for breast cancer, heart disease, or uterine cancer.

If you didn't make decisions about your bone health before menopause concluded, it's not too late. The sooner you start supporting your bone health, the better your bones will be able to carry you into the later years of life.

In addition to your bones, HRT after menopause can have beneficial effects on your vagina, bladder, and urinary tract, and on your skin and hair. Every woman must weigh the risks of taking HRT long term against the benefits, especially when natural alternatives can provide many of the same health-enhancing effects without the risks.

Whether or not you choose to take HRT long term, making lifestyle changes that encourage and support overall good health will enhance your self-image and self-esteem, adding the vitality that can make everything you do in life more rewarding.

Question 6

If I'm on HRT, Should I Stop Immediately in Light of the New Findings? And What Is the Best Way to Stop?

When the media released the news that the Women's Health Initiative (WHI) study was abruptly stopped because it was determined that the risks were too great for the women taking the estrogen/progestin HRT Prempro to continue, telephones in doctors' offices around the country started ringing endlessly. Women on HRT were panicking, and rightly so.

The news headlines were daunting, indeed. It was a wake-up call for millions of women who take some kind of HRT (38 percent of postmenopausal women in the United States.) In fact, 22.6 million prescriptions were written for Prempro in 2000, and 46 million were written for its estrogen-only sister drug Premarin, which is the second most frequently prescribed medication in the United States (with $1 billion in sales).

As if the headlines weren't bad enough, reading the actual results of the study published in the July 17, 2002, issue of the *Journal of the*

American Medical Association could make many woman want to toss their hormones into the trash.

In fact, it isn't as bad at it seemed at first glance, but it also isn't that good.

The truth is, it's probably time for most women to go back to where they started: trying to make the hormone decision. But this time the decision is, should you stop immediately?

The Women's Health Initiative Study of Estrogen/Progestin HRT

Data from the WHI study basically comes down to this: If you are a woman who has completed menopause, if you still have your uterus, if you are still healthy, and if you are taking estrogen/progestin HRT, you have an increased risk of developing invasive breast cancer, heart disease, or blood clots, or having a stroke. The risks are very small, but still they are risks.

On the other hand, the estrogen/progestin HRT decreases your risk of developing colon cancer (although they don't know why), osteoporosis, and bone fractures, including hip fractures.

What Is the Women's Health Initiative?

The Women's Health Initiative (WHI) is the name given to a set of clinical studies and an observational study sponsored by the National Heart, Lung, and Blood Institute in collaboration with the National Institutes of Health. The WHI's focus is to define the risks and benefits of strategies that could potentially reduce the incidence of heart disease, breast and colorectal cancer, and fractures in postmenopausal women.

Between 1993 and 1998, the WHI recruited 161,809 healthy post-menopausal women to participate in some clinical studies, two of them on postmenopausal hormone use. Their estrogen/progestin HRT randomized, controlled, primary prevention clinical study included 16,608 of those women (from forty U.S. clinical centers) who had not had hysterectomies. Half of the group was given the HRT, and the other half was given a placebo, a pill that looks like the real HRT but has no biologic effect. The study had two main goals: first to see if the HRT would help prevent heart disease and hip fractures; and second, if the former proved to be true, to see if the heart disease benefits were greater than the possible risks for breast cancer, endometrial cancer, and blood clots.

The fifteen-year study was supposed to end in 2005, giving the WHI an 8.5-year picture of the effects of estrogen/progestin HRT (conjugated equine estrogens, 0.625 mg/day, plus medroxyprogesterone acetate, 2.5 mg/day, in one tablet) on the health of healthy postmenopausal women in a wide age range. But after 5.2 years of follow-up on the participants' health, it was determined that the study should be stopped because the risks of taking the HRT outweighed and outnumbered the benefits.

Another WHI study, focusing on collecting clinical data about the health of women who have had hysterectomies and are taking estrogen alone, continues as planned. The results of that study are expected in 2005.

Why Was the Estrogen/Progestin HRT Study Stopped?

Follow-up data on the participants' health was collected and analyzed every six months. During the most recent review, two determinations were made:

1. Among the women taking the estrogen/progestin HRT, there was a 26 percent higher incidence of invasive breast cancer than among the placebo group of women.[1] This is what caused the study to be stopped.

   During the first four years of the study there was no difference in the development of breast cancer in the woman taking the HRT, as compared to those taking the placebo pill. The numbers changed after that time. At around 5.2 years into the study, the increased risk of breast cancer showed up in the women taking the HRT but not those taking the placebo.
2. Among the women taking the estrogen/progestin, the risks of heart attack, strokes, and blood clots to the lungs and legs outweighed the benefits of HRT, despite the fact that HDL (good cholesterol) increased and LDL (bad cholesterol) decreased.

These two factors alone met the criterion originally agreed upon for safety when the study was devised: If the risks outweighed the benefits, the study would be stopped. Although the heart attack risk had stabilized by 5.2 years, during the first year of the study it had increased before going back down and stabilizing. Considering the increase in invasive breast cancer rates that occurred at 5.2 years, statistically there was nothing to gain by continuing the study because the numbers could never have returned to showing benefits outweighing risks.

The following statistics have been released for the study. They are calculated to be for a one-year period, for every 10,000 women taking estrogen/progestin:

1. The WHI is emphasizing that these increases in risk appear high because the are risks to a population of 10,000; the actual risk to an individual is very small, perhaps as low as 1/10 of 1 percent.

Breast cancer: For every 10,000 women taking the HRT, thirty-eight developed breast cancer compared to thirty who were taking the placebo, a 26 percent increased risk.

Heart attacks: for every 10,000 women taking the HRT, thirty-seven had heart attacks, compared to thirty women who were taking the placebo, a 29 percent increased risk

Strokes: for every 10,000 women taking the HRT, twenty-nine had strokes, compared to twenty-one women who were taking the placebo, a 41 percent increased risk.

Blood clots in the lungs or legs: For every 10,000 women taking the HRT, thirty-four had blood clots, compared to sixteen who were taking the placebo, a 112 percent increased risk.

On the other hand, among the women taking the estrogen/progestin HRT, there was no change in endometrial (uterine) cancer, fewer women suffered bone and hip fractures, and fewer developed colorectal cancer (although they don't know why).

Colorectal cancer: There was a 37 percent decrease in colorectal cancer among the women taking the HRT, as compared to the placebo group.

Hip fractures: There was a 34 percent decreased risk.

Total fractures: There was a 24 percent decreased risk.

What Estrogen/Progestin HRT Was Used in the Study?

The actual hormones used in the trial were Prempro conjugated equine estrogens, 0.625 mg, and medroxyprogesterone acetate, 2.5 mg, daily. This particular hormone combination was selected because it is the most commonly prescribed HRT for women with an intact uterus.

Does the WHI Say If Women Should Stop Taking Their HRT?

The WHI does not address that question directly. Their general recommendation to physicians is that estrogen/progestin therapy "should not be continued or started to prevent heart disease."

On their Web site they suggest that women who are taking estrogen/progestin HRT should talk with their health care providers about their individual health-risk profile and how it may be affected by the hormones they are currently taking.

When the WHI closed down the study, the participants were asked to stop taking their study pills and told that they would be informed of their former study pill assignment. They were told to stop taking their pills because as the data was being analyzed the WHI saw an increased risk of breast cancer in women taking estrogen/progestin and also saw that the previously identified risks for heart attacks, strokes, and blood clots to the lungs and legs had persisted. After assessing this information, the board of the WHI decided that the overall risks outweighed the benefits of taking estrogen/progestin.

Some other general recommendations by the WHI include the following:

- They suggest women consult their physicians about other methods of preventing heart disease, such as lifestyle changes and medications to lower cholesterol or blood pressure.
- Women concerned about osteoporosis prevention are directed to consult with their physicians and weigh the benefits of taking estrogen/progestin HRT against their own personal risks for heart attack, stroke, blood clots, and breast

cancer. They say that alternative treatments for osteoporosis and bone fractures are also available.

- Most importantly, women are encouraged to continue having their regularly scheduled mammograms and routinely conduct breast self-exams.

What If I Am Taking Low Doses or Other Formulations of Estrogen/Progestin HRT?

The WHI says the estrogen/progestin study results may not apply to women taking lower doses of HRT or to other estrogen and progestin formulations. They also say they can't make specific recommendations about other hormone medications, such as different estrogens or progestins, or about hormones women take in lower dosages or in different ways, such as patches instead of pills. They note, however, without scientific clinical trial data, one cannot assume that alternative estrogen plus progestin treatments are any safer than those in the study. Finally, they say they cannot make any conclusions about phytoestrogens because they haven't studied them.

What If I Am Taking HRT During My Menopausal Transition?

Although the WHI did not study the short-term use of estrogen/progestin HRT for relief of menopausal symptoms, they say it may reap more benefits than risks. Still, women should talk with their physicians about the risks before deciding.

If I Decide to Stop Taking HRT

After carefully reconsidering whether the benefits of HRT outweigh the risks for your body, if you do decide to stop, this is how you can do it.

Keep in mind that it's not a good idea to go on and off HRT. When you stop taking HRT, it has an effect on your entire body.

How Should I Stop Taking HRT?

If you've been taking HRT for a short time and decide to stop, you can just stop. However, if you've been taking HRT for an extended period of time, it's better to wean yourself gradually from the drugs by reducing dosages. Either way, you should discuss this with your physician, who will help you devise the best plan for you personally.

Gradually stopping sometimes involves skipping either days or weeks. Or your doctor may suggest it is better to systematically lower your prescription dosage over time before you skip days. If you are using a skin patch, your doctor may suggest you wear it for gradually shorter periods of time and less often.

How Will My Body React If I Stop Taking HRT?

If you stop taking HRT, you could experience the physical discomforts of menopause if your body was never given the opportunity to make its own natural hormonal adjustments at the time of your menopause. Some of the natural changes in your body that would have occurred after menopause, but were offset by HRT, will begin.

Most importantly, you may lose bone mass during the few years immediately following withdrawal from HRT. This may be your most serious concern if you are at risk of developing osteoporosis.

There are numerous ways to offset the side effects of HRT withdrawal. Other chapters in this book provide suggestions, aside from HRT, on how to support the health of your body.

Finally, continue to monitor your own health and get regular medical checkups and examinations.

Conclusion

The purpose of the WHI study was to determine whether HRT is a viable long-term preventive treatment strategy that can benefit the overall health of postmenopausal women who are still healthy. Numerous other studies have been conducted on postmenopausal women with existing health problems or those who have already suffered serious health episodes. Among the most respected of the studies completed to date, most have reached the same conclusions about estrogen/progestin HRT:

- The risk of developing breast cancer becomes increasingly greater the longer you take estrogen/progestin HRT.
- Bone fractures and colon cancer risks are reduced when you take estrogen/progestin HRT.
- The risks of stroke and blood clots continue throughout the time you are taking HRT.
- Coronary heart disease is usually elevated the first year you take estrogen/progestin HRT, but then it reduces and levels off.

Because the WHI study of estrogen alone taken by women without a uterus continues uninterrupted after over 5.2 years, it is assumed that the data coming in so far indicates that it may be beneficial for otherwise healthy women to take estrogen alone if they have no uterus.

According to Drs. Suzanne W. Fletcher and Graham A. Colditz:

> [T]he whole purpose of healthy women taking long-term estrogen/progestin therapy is to preserve health and prevent disease. The results of [the WHI] study provide strong evidence that the opposite is happening for important aspects of women's health, even if the absolute risk is low.

These statements were contained in an article reviewing the WHI study in the July 17, 2002, issue of the *Journal of the American Medical Association*, a publication through which doctors speak to their peers. There may be other professional opinions about the WHI study and its recommendations. Doctors are still trying to sort out all the information, just as you are.

As you are reassessing your hormone decision, all the facts and all of these opinions can be considered, along with the opinion of your own physician. However, in the end the decision to continue taking HRT or to stop is yours alone to make.

Question 7

What Else Can I Do to Enhance My Overall Health, With or Without HRT?

You know how much better you feel when you eat a healthy, nutritious diet, get routine, moderate exercise, and avoid unhealthy activities. No question about it, your lifestyle affects your health, both physical and emotional.

Now is the time to consider whether your lifestyle is affecting the quality of your menopause as well, and how your lifestyle may even help you decide whether you need to take HRT.

If your risk factors are low enough for you to have decided it is safe and beneficial for you to be taking HRT, your lifestyle choices could improve the effectiveness of the HRT you've chosen, perhaps even lowering your dosage. Besides, most doctors will tell you that HRT alone, without adequate nutritional intake and a routine exercise program, cannot prevent every serious health problem that a woman can develop later in life.

Following these general guidelines will enhance your overall health and can make your menopausal transition much easier, with or without HRT:

- Drink lots of fresh, toxin-free water.
- Adjust your diet and nutritional intake, gradually eliminating foods that are detrimental to your health and increasing health-affirming foods.
- Take nutritional supplements and/or herbs when needed, based on your individual health profile and your nutritional food intake.
- Undertake a routine, moderate exercise program of at least thirty minutes every day or sixty minutes every other day.
- Learn how to reduce harmful stress in your life.
- Adopt effective techniques to help you deal with the harmful stress you can't eliminate.
- Try to avoid self-imposed toxic exposure (cigarette smoking and excessive alcohol consumption) and environmental toxins (heavy metals, chemicals, and pesticides) as much as possible.
- Seek professional health care support and assistance when you need it.

Water

Water may be the most overlooked antidote to aging. Our bodies—at least 75 percent water—require constant replenishment of this essential fluid. Every cell of your body needs water for hydrating skin, regulating body temperature, lubricating, flushing waste and toxins, and transporting nutrients so your body can maintain its balance and support all its functions. Adequate water intake helps your skin stay smooth and prevents tiny wrinkles from forming. Because water flushes the bladder, it often reduces the likelihood of urinary tract infections.

It has been recommended that you drink at least six to eight glasses of clean, pure water every day to maintain optimal health. Water intake should be increased during hot weather in order to rehydrate your body, even when you don't feel thirsty.

Tap water is generally not considered beneficial for optimal health, although the quality of tap water varies from city to city. Most city water is processed and treated in order to remove harmful elements (although some viruses and bacteria survive) and in the process chlorine and fluoride are added, which some experts believe are harmful to health and may contribute to bone loss associated with osteoporosis.

Bottled water is better. Distilled water, the purest, is widely advocated for use during healing programs. However, continuous use of distilled water over long periods of time may deplete the body of minerals and requires supplementary mineral intake to resupply the body. Purified water is similar to distilled water.

Natural mineral waters contain minerals that are beneficial to the body and must come from a protected underground source. Spring water comes from an underground source that could flow naturally to the surface but is usually pumped into containers. Artesian water comes from natural wells in rock formations and is pumped out so that it does not come in contact with possible toxins in the soil while being bottled. Natural sparkling water contains natural carbonation and is a good replacement for carbonated sodas.

Sparkling water has CO_2 added to make it fizzy. Club soda is tap water with CO_2 added for fizz and mineral salts added for flavor. Seltzer is tap water with CO_2 added for fizz but is usually salt free because no mineral salts are added. Flavored waters may come from either a natural source or the tap and could have either natural or artificial flavors, as well as sugar or sweeteners.

Dietary Habits

Especially during menopause and immediately afterward when your body is still adjusting to hormonal changes, it's important to eliminate foods and beverages that are detrimental to your health and to add foods and beverages that are beneficial for your body. Providing your body with nutritional support enhances your vitality and increases your body's recuperative abilities during this time of dramatic physical changes. Gradually changing your dietary habits increases your chances of making permanent changes that can reinforce your health into your later years of life.

Coffee, strong black tea, and sodas are generally considered harmful to the body, except in moderation. Although alcohol consumption is debated, there is no question that excessive alcohol is detrimental. Some medical experts believe a glass or two of wine or a beer daily is beneficial to health, but that depends on the individual and her personal and family health profiles.

Most processed sodas, cola drinks, and sweetened, carbonated beverages not only contain large amounts of sugar or artificial sweeteners, which are known to be bad for the body, but also contain phosphorus, which leaches calcium from the bones. This is a particular concern for women during and after menopause when bone loss can accelerate due to lower levels of hormone production.

Coffee, black tea, and some sodas also contain large amounts of caffeine. Although caffeine in various forms has been used throughout history as a beneficial stimulant, it is the form and quantity in which it is taken into the body that is important. Caffeine naturally provides energy, raises body temperature, suppresses appetite, and increases metabolism. But excessive consumption of caffeine can become an addictive stimulant. It can raise blood pressure and cause heart palpitations, anxiety and nervousness, digestive and stomach problems, headaches, and sleep disturbance. It can leach vitamins and minerals from the body, contributing to hormonal imbalances and osteoporosis. Caffeine has been linked to breast and uterine fibroid tumors, PMS, heart disease, and high cholesterol.

Your accumulated caffeine consumption may be higher than you think when you consider the numerous sources of caffeine. Both coffee and tea have large amounts of caffeine. Smaller quantities of caffeine can have a cumulative effect on the body when you consume certain soft drinks, some pain medications, and chocolate, which contains a caffeinelike substance.

If you decide to eliminate caffeine totally from your diet, it's best to do so gradually; otherwise you may experience withdrawal symptoms, such as severe headaches that can last for several days. Gradually reducing caffeine consumption would probably be in the best health interest of all women.

What Food Adjustments Are Good for My Body During and After Menopause?

Foods that are detrimental to your health include refined flours and processed foods, animal fats, and sugar. Your overall health will benefit most from eating fresh, whole, natural foods, including grains, nuts, seeds, vegetables, fruits, fish, and poultry.

Food in its natural, fresh form is filled with nutrients that are lost when it's refined and processed. The most significant amounts of vitamins and minerals in grains are in the germ and bran, and these are usually removed during the milling process that produces flour. It has been estimated that 30 percent of the average diet consists of grains, usually as refined flour. That is a substantial loss of potential vitamin and mineral consumption in the diet, especially during the middle and later years of life when the body needs extra nutritional support.

Processed food has usually been exposed to high temperatures, radiation, or chemicals and may need to be reshaped to give it texture. Artificial colors, flavors, and preservatives may be added to make it look good, taste good, and last a long time on the supermarket shelf. At this point, if it has any nutritional value, it's most likely because vitamins and minerals have been put back in unnaturally. The end product is food that may look, feel, and taste real, but it's been manufactured. It may supply nutrients to your body, but not as natural balanced foods can in their original form, with amino acids intact. Further, any chemicals used in food processing and preserving, flavoring, and coloring are foreign substances to your body.

A well-balanced diet of fresh foods is more likely to furnish your body with all the elements it needs to stay healthy during the menopausal transition and into your later years of life: protein, complex carbohydrates, soluble fiber, vitamins, minerals, and amino acids.

Protein strengthens your body and enhances healing. Complex carbohydrates provide energy and stamina. Soluble fiber helps your body discard waste and toxins, assisting in weight management. Vitamins, minerals, and amino acids are the essential elements for your body to energize and renew itself by stimulating the body's metabolism and helping it convert protein and carbohydrates into tissue and energy.

Is Any Particular Food Especially Beneficial During Menopause?

Because some foods have an estrogenic effect in the body, they may help to alleviate discomforts of menopause, making it unnecessary for you to take HRT or enable you to take a lower dosage. For example, soybeans (which contain phytoestrogens) and soy foods such as tofu, miso, koridofu, aburage, and atuage are generously eaten in Japan, where women rarely have menopausal symptoms. Other foods that have an estrogenic effect in the body and have been shown to be beneficial for relieving the discomforts of menopause are alfalfa, almonds, apples, cashew nuts, corn, cucumbers, oats, peanuts, peas, and wheat.

Vitamins and Minerals

Vitamins E, B_6, B_{12}, PABA, folic acid, and pantothenic acid have an estrogenic effect in the body. If you are taking these vitamins, or wish to, and are taking HRT, please discuss with your doctor whether your dosage needs to be adjusted.

The advice of a health care professional with training in nutrition can help you tailor your nutritional intake and supplemental vitamin/mineral dosages to your individual health needs. The following vitamins and minerals have been found to benefit women during their middle and later years:

- Vitamin A is found in apricots, broccoli, cantaloupe, carrots, lettuce, parsley, spinach, turnips, fish, and dairy products. It's good for the mucous membranes, reproductive system, skin, and eyes; is required for cell regeneration, regulation of hormone synthesis, and cartilage formation; and supports liver and adrenal gland functions. Vitamin A is an antioxidant. It helps your body by enabling it to handle stress and resist infection.

  Do not take vitamin A supplements if you are taking birth control pills or HRT. Women taking these medications usually have increased levels of vitamin A and do not need to supplement. Vitamin A is also unnecessary if you are taking cod liver oil or fish oil supplements, which contain high levels of the vitamin. Also avoid vitamin A supplements if you're taking the drug Accutane (isotretinoin), which is made from vitamin A, for a skin condition.

- Vitamin B complex (twenty different vitamins are included), which is found in almonds, brewer's yeast, salmon and other fish, meat and liver, and wheat germ, is essential for almost every function of the body. It is often suggested that women take vitamin B complex supplements, especially during and after menopause.
- B_5 (calcium pantothenate, pantothenic acid) is found in brewer's yeast, green vegetables, eggs, meat, nuts, wheat germ and bran, and whole grains. It reduces stress and aids adrenal function (estrogen production shifts from the ovaries to the adrenals at menopause).
- B_6 (pyridoxine) is found in blackstrap molasses, brewer's yeast, cantaloupe, cabbage, eggs, fish, meat, milk, peanuts, soybeans, walnuts, wheat bran, and wheat germ. It has a progesterone effect in your body, decreasing water retention and menopausal symptoms. More is needed if you are taking estrogen.
- Vitamin C is found in broccoli, brussels sprouts, cauliflower, citrus fruits, green leafy vegetables, parsley, peppers, potatoes, and strawberries. It is important for regeneration of body cells, is beneficial to your cardiovascular system, and can alleviate hot flashes.
- Vitamin D, which is naturally manufactured by your body during exposure to sunlight, is also found in fish, fish oils, milk, and dairy products. Vitamin D is important for healthy bones.
- Vitamin E is found in bee pollen, cold-pressed oils, eggs, green vegetables, peanuts, soybeans, wheat germ, and whole grains. It is beneficial for your reproductive organs, cardiovascular sys-

tem, nerves, muscles, and skin. Vitamin E can relieve vaginal dryness and itching. Also, along with B complex, it relieves hot flashes and other discomforts associated with menopause, including emotional symptoms.

Precaution: If you have rheumatic heart disease, please discuss with your physician if it is necessary for you to limit your vitamin E intake and avoid vitamin E supplements.

While taking HRT, vitamin E with selenium is recommended. However, vitamin E stimulates estrogen in your body; therefore, it needs to be taken several hours before or after HRT. Taking vitamin E may enhance the effectiveness of HRT, so please discuss with your doctor whether your HRT dosage should be adjusted.

To relieve vaginal dryness, puncture a capsule of vitamin E and insert a few drops into your vagina.

- Vitamin F (essential fatty acid) is found in virgin cold-pressed oils such as canola, corn, linseed, peanut, safflower, sesame, sunflower, and walnut, as well as in avocados, almonds, peanuts, pecans, sunflower seeds, and walnuts. Essential fatty acids (EFAs) are important for estrogen production, act as a sedative and diuretic, and aid in alleviating hot flashes. EFAs are essential for cell regeneration and are an antitoxin, benefiting your circulation, liver, nerves, and skin. EFAs are contained in supplements of evening primrose oil, black currant oil, and flaxseed oil.

The following minerals are usually recommended for women during and after menopause:

- Calcium is found in almonds, green vegetables, dairy products, and sesame seeds. It can alleviate hot flashes when used with vitamin C. Because calcium benefits the nervous system, it can help alleviate emotional symptoms of menopause, such as anxiety and depression, and it contributes to better sleep and relaxation. Calcium and magnesium are essential for bone health, with added boron.

- Iron is found in apricots, eggs, molasses, parsley, red beets, spinach, and whole grains. It is an essential element of healthy blood and necessary to avoid anemia, especially if you are experiencing profuse menstrual bleeding.
- Copper, found in fresh fruits and green vegetables, is necessary for iron to be absorbed by your body.
- Magnesium is found in eggs, lemons, milk, nuts, sea salt, soy products, and whole grains. It is essential for your body to absorb calcium. It has an antiaging effect by supporting cell regeneration, relieves hot flashes, and calms nerves.
- Selenium is a trace mineral and antioxidant taken daily in amounts ranging from 50 to 200 mcg. Studies have shown a connection between selenium deficiency and the pain and swelling of arthritis. Studies have also indicated that breast cancer patients often have selenium deficiencies.

If you're eating all the right foods and taking supplements that don't seem to be working, or if your stomach is having difficulty adjusting to your change of diet, acidophilus and digestive enzymes may help.

- Acidophilus enables the intestines to absorb nutrients by supporting and maintaining your body's production of beneficial bacteria. It is contained in cultured food, such as yogurt, kefir, and some types of milk. Supplements are available at health food stores. Acidophilus capsules can be inserted into your vagina at night to help prevent or alleviate vaginal infections.

- Digestive enzymes, including HCl (hydrochloric acid), are essential for the body to assimilate nutrients. Although they are contained in all unprocessed, uncooked foods, it may be necessary to supplement your diet, especially with HCl. Many combination vitamin/mineral formulations contain HCl.

If I Eat Enough Nutritious Foods, Do I Need to Take Vitamins, Too?

Most women cannot get enough vital nutrients from today's food because it is grown in nutrient-depleted soil and exposed to toxins from groundwater contamination, pesticides, and chemical fertilizers. Further, processed and junk food diets not only do not provide nutrients to your body, they also deplete your body of stored nutrients.

Even if you're taking good supplements, a nutritious diet is still necessary. Although supplements can be beneficial, they do not contain the complex nutrient balance of fresh, wholesome food. Supplements are not as easily assimilated by the body as the nutrients in fresh food. When taken in safe amounts, supplements are not stored by the body for use when they are needed but are excreted in the urine. Studies have shown that taking lower doses of nutritional supplements, along with a nutritious, healthy diet, can reduce your risks of heart attack and osteoporosis later in life.

Exercise

Exercise has an antiaging effect on your body. It strengthens muscles and bones, benefits the cardiovascular system, lowers cholesterol levels, helps regulate weight, increases energy, reduces stress, and improves mental attitude. Regular, moderate weight-bearing exercise is best.

Walking at a quick pace for half an hour every day or one hour every other day is the most widely recommended form of exercise. Yoga is an excellent form of exercise that tones and stretches muscles as it provides aerobic benefits. Tennis and stair climbing are also good. Aerobic exercise routines such as bicycling and swimming are good but need to be combined with appropriate weight-bearing exercise to be beneficial for your bones.

Excessive aerobic exercise that lowers body fat to abnormal levels is detrimental to the hormonal balance of a woman's body and can contribute to early menopause.

If you have any symptoms of heart disease, please consult a physician before you begin any exercise routine other than walking.

Stress Management

Not all stress is bad. Stress can motivate us, challenge us, and inspire us. And we know that our bodies need to be stressed and stimulated in order to remain strong and healthy.

But stress begins to affect us negatively when our minds tell our bodies we cannot handle it. Our muscles and organs tense up, our breathing becomes shallow, and our blood flow is altered; the mind then sends signals to the rest of the body that something is out of balance.

When we are in balance, our glands secrete hormones that regenerate and renew the body. But when we are feeling stressed, our glands are overstimulated, releasing extra hormones in an attempt to regain balance within the body. In turn, the body needs more nutritional support and too quickly utilizes the available nutrients. If adequate nutrients are not made available to the body through our food intake and supplements, the body will draw the nutrients it needs from the body's warehouses, especially from bones.

All of this can lead to additional hormonal imbalances, causing more discomfort during menopause; vitamin, mineral, and nutritional deficiencies within the body; and an extra load on the entire body, especially the glands, cardiovascular system, and bones.

A feeling of well-being is important for women, especially during menopause when they are experiencing more physical changes than at any time during their lives since puberty. A positive outlook is very important. Women who take time for daily grooming feel better about themselves and are generally happier and more relaxed about life.

Some doctors prescribe tranquilizers for women who are overwrought during menopause. But there are numerous nondrug therapies that can help to relieve stress, as well as relaxation techniques you can learn.

Along with dietary changes, vitamins, minerals, and exercise routines discussed earlier in this chapter, here are some other ways you can reduce or better manage harmful stress:

- Acupressure can be self-applied to some parts of your body to reduce tension, as well as to relieve menopausal discomforts.
- Biofeedback is a stress reduction and relaxation technique widely used by both conventional and alternative medical communities. An electronic machine is connected to sensors applied to your skin. The sensors measure your skin temperature and electrical responses while a visual display shows you the effect that tension and anxiety have on your body. Once

you learn to recognize tension, you are taught techniques to change your responses, thus controlling stress effects on your body. Biofeedback is an effective relaxation technique that can help you overcome anxiety, headaches, and insomnia.

- Dance therapy can help you express your emotions while releasing tension in your body and mind. The therapeutic effects of music enhance the activity.
- Deep breathing: When you become aware of your body or mind becoming tense, taking several long, deep breaths will help you relax. Each time you breathe out, focus on feeling your muscles becoming looser and softer.
- Hypnotherapy is a partnership treatment between a patient and doctor that allows the doctor to induce a state of suspended brain function in the region of the brain linked to anxiety, blood pressure, and emotions. While in the suspended state, you can be taught to change the way your brain responds to everyday situations. Studies have shown it helps people feel more relaxed, stop smoking, lose weight, feel less pain, and heal faster.
- Massage relaxes the body by releasing stress in the muscles. Massage is especially effective because it is a period of time to totally surrender your body and energy to a massage therapist who does all the work for you. It can also be effective in helping your body correct imbalances that lead to menopausal discomforts.
- Meditation and prayer can calm your mind and your body, and enhance healing.
- Reflexology can be performed by a massage therapist, reflexologist, or yourself by pressing points on the feet or hands. It relaxes, releases stress from, and can adjust imbalances in your body during menopause.

- Visualization and guided imagery are based on the theory that the mind controls the body. You can learn to visualize changes in your body from an unhealthy state to a healthy condition. The technique has been used throughout the history of medicine to quiet the mind and reduce stress, and is believed to lead to faster healing. Studies have shown that guided imagery (visualization) is being used successfully by some cancer patients to shrink their tumors and by people with persistent infections because it appears to boost the body's immune activity. It is also widely used by athletes to improve their performance.
- Yoga, meaning "union" in Sanskrit, assists in integrating the body, emotions, mind, and spirit. Although there are several types of yoga, the variety most commonly and easily practiced in the West is Hatha yoga. As you stretch and tone the muscles in slow, relaxed positions, the effects of gravity are counteracted, improving your posture and balance, and giving you a feeling of well-being. Because many of the positions increase circulation, yoga can have an aerobic effect as well. Deep breathing and meditation often accompany yoga, enhancing your sense of self and giving you an opportunity to look inward and feel at peace.

Conclusion

Transitional times of life offer us a wonderful opportunity to view the past, present, and future in rapid succession. During the menopausal years your body speaks to you, telling you how your lifestyle has either contributed to your current good health or created challenges for you to endure. Few women pass through menopause without understanding clearly what their bodies are telling them.

During this time when you are, no doubt, receiving clear messages from your body, consider with wisdom the choices you will make from this moment on and how your body will respond today, tomorrow, and during all the years ahead of you.

Resources

Natural Hormones

To find information on natural progesterone, estriol, and referrals to physicians familiar with natural hormones:

John Lee, M.D.
The definitive expert on natural progesterone
www.johnleemd.com

Matol
The makers of Bonanelle Progesterone Cream
Botanical International, Quebec, Canada
514-639-3347
www.matol.com

Pure Essence Labs
The makers of Femcream
Henderson, NV
1-800-264-8000

Vitamin Research Products, Inc.
The makers of HerBalance Cream
Carson City, NV
1-800-877-2477
www.vrp.com

Women's Medicine, Inc.
Makers of Dr. Randy Randolph's Cream, Natural Balance Progesta-Fem Progesterone Cream, which contains chemical-free progesterone as its active ingredient (600 mg of progesterone per ounce of cream)
www.womensmedicine.com

Compounding Pharmacies

These pharmacies will work with your doctor to compound natural hormones to meet your needs. Most will refer you to doctors in your area who are familiar with natural hormones.

ApotheCure
Dallas, TX
1-800-969-6601
www.apothecure.com

People's Pharmacy
Austin, TX
www.healthcarecentral.com/peoplesrx.com

Women's International Pharmacy
Madison, WI
1-800-279-5708
www.womensinternational.com

A directory of compounding pharmacies can be found at www.dmoz.org/health/pharmacies/compounding

Websites

Various websites to find information relating to your health care and lifestyle choices, including alternative health care:

American College for the Advance of Medicine
Updates physicians on the latest alternative medicine
www.acam.org

Alternative Medicine Digest
A one-stop information site by *Alternative Medicine Digest*
www.alternativemedicine.com

The Center for Food Safety
Sponsored by the Food and Drug Administration. Provides information and consumer advice on labeling, nutrition and dietary supplements, pesticides, and lead in food.
www.cfsan.fda.gov/list.html

Citizens for Health: Defending Your Right to Choose
A very pro-active grass roots organization advocating protection and expansion of consumer health choices
www.citizens.org

The Life Sciences Institute of Body-Mind Health
Offers information about self-regulation of mind and body by using biofeedback, visualization, imagery, and other procedures.
www.cjnetworks.com/~lifesci

Families First
Information about mood disorders associated with hormone imbalances
www.families-first.com/hotflash/faw/serotonin.htm

The American Society for Clinical Nutrition
The latest information on nutrition
www.faseb.org/ascn

Fluoride Action Network (FAN)
An international coalition to end water fluoridation, provides information and news updates about the health effects and environmental risks of fluoride.
www.fluoridealert.org

Healing Edge
A resource for alternative health information and consultations with health care professionals. Also sells high-quality natural supplements, such as vitamins and minerals, and a wide range of homeopathic remedies.
www.healingedge.net

Herb Research Foundation
A nonprofit educational and research group on medicinal plants and herbs. Also copublisher of *Herbalgram* magazine.
www.herbs.org

Howdy Neighbor
Devoted to the topic of menopause, this Web site is visited by many alternative health practitioners.
www.howdyneighbor.com/menopaus

Medscape
Medical Web site for medical professionals, with a wide range of the latest medical news, resources and links. You will have to register to obtain access.
www.medscape.com

The National Institutes of Health (NIH)
National Library of Medicine
At this Web site you can research almost any medical topic. This is also where you can find the Women's Health Initiative Web site.
www.nim.nih.gov

On Health
Provides the latest health news, as well as reports on local pollen and air quality
www.onhealth.com

Power Surge
This huge menopause Web site has an upbeat attitude while presenting resources and educational materials, including a library of interview transcripts.
www.power-surge.com

The Association of Women for the Advancement of Research and Education (AWARE)
A nonprofit organization dedicated to providing comprehensive information to enable premenopausal and menopausal women to make informed choices about their health care options,

including resources, therapies, and research data
www.project-aware.org

Women's Health—About.com guide
A huge Web site providing a wealth of information about every aspect of women's health
www.womenshealth.about.com

The Institute for Women's Leadership
Provides training, coaching, and resources for women, encouraging them to make powerful contributions as leaders in their organizations and communities, while leading authentic and fulfilling lives
www.womensleadership.com

Books, Publications, and Products

Various books and publications that provide information about healthcare, including natural and alternative healthcare.

Acupressure

Acupressure's Potent Points: A Guide to Self-Care for Common Ailments
By Michael Reed, Bantam Doubleday Dell Publications, 1990

Aromatherapy

Aromatherapy 101
By Karen Downes, Hay House, 2000

The Healing Power of Aromatherapy
By Asnain Walji, Prima Publishing, 1996

Ayurvedic Medicine

A Woman's Best Medicine for Menopause: Your Personal Guide to Radiant Good Health Using Maharishi Ayurveda
By Nancy K. Lonsdorf, M.D., Contemporary Books, 2002

Bach Flower Remedies

Bach Flower Remedies
By Edward Heal Thyself Bach (editor), Edward Twelve Bach, and F. J. Wheeler (contributor), Contemporary Books, 1998

Breast Cancer Prevention

The Breast Sourcebook
By M. Sara Rosenthal, Contemporary Books, 2000

What Your Doctor May Not Tell You About Breast Cancer
By John R. Lee, M.D., David Zava, Ph.D., and Virginia Hopkins, Warner Books, 2002

Herbalism

The Healing Herbs: The Ultimate Guide to the Curative Powers of Nature's Medicine
By Michael Castleman, Rodale Press, 1991

The Healing Power of Herbs. The Enlightened Person's Guide to the Wonders of Medicinal Plants
By Michael Murray, Prima Publishing, 1995

Heart Health

Dr. Dean Ornish's Program for Reversing Heart Disease: The Only System Scientifically Proven to Reverse Heart Disease Without Drugs or Surgery
By Dean Ornish, M.D., Ivy Books, 1996

Healing from the Heart: A Leading Surgeon Combines Eastern and Western Traditions to Create the Medicine of the Future
By Mehmet Oz, M.D., Lisa Oz, and Mehmet C. Oz, Plume, 1999

Homeopathy

Everybody's Guide to Homeopathic Medicines: Safe, Effective Remedies for You and Your Family
By Stephen Cummings and Dana Ullman, J. P. Tarcher, 1997

Menopause & Homeopathy: A Guide for Women in Midlife
By Ifeoma Ikenze and Afeome Akenze, North Atlantic Books, 1998

Menopause

As We Change, a catalogue of menopause-related products.
1-800-203-5585
www.aswechange.com

Stress Management

Stress Relief & Relaxation Techniques
By Judith Lazarus, Contemporary Books, 2000

Thyroid Health

The Thyroid Sourcebook
By M. Sara Rosenthal, Contemporary Books, 2000

Women's Health

A Friend Indeed Publications, Inc.
Pembina, ND
204-989-8028 or 204-989-8029 (fax)
afi@pangea.ca or
http://www.afriendindeed.ca
Menopause-related newsletter for a subscription fee.

The Gynechological Sourcebook
By M. Sara Rosenthal, Contemporary Books, 1999

Menopause and the Mind: The Complete Guide to Coping with Cognitive Effects of Perimenopause and Menopause, Including Memory Loss, Foggy Thinking, Verbal Confusion, and Verbal Slips.
By Claire L. Warga, Ph.D., Touchstone Books, 2000

What Your Doctor May Not Tell You About Premenopause
By John R. Lee, M.D., and Jesse Hanley, M.D., Warner Books, 1999
www.johnleemd.com

What Your Doctor May Not Tell You About Menopause
By John R. Lee, M.D. with Virginia Hopkins, Warner Books, 1999
www.johnleemd.com

Yoga

Yoga Journal
www.yogajournal.com
Magazine available at newsstands. Lists classes and workshops nationwide.

To Find Health Practitioners

Acupuncture

American Academy of Medical Acupuncture
323-937-5514
www.medicalacupuncture.org

American Association of Acupuncture & Oriental Medicine
1-888-550-7999
www.aaom.org

Ayurvedic Medicine

Maharishi Ayurveda Health Center for Stress Management and Behavioral Medicine
508-365-4549
www.concerningwomen.com/wl_article2.html

Ayurvedic Institute
505-291-9698

Biofeedback

American Association of Biofeedback Clinicians
312-827-0440

Association for Applied Psychophysiology & Biofeedback
www.aapb.org/links

Cardiovascular Health

American Heart Association
1-800-242-8721

American Stroke Association
1-888-478-7653
www.americanheart.org

Chinese Herbalism (See also Acupuncture)

American College of Traditional Chinese Medicine
415-282-7600
www.actcm.org

Chiropractic

American Chiropractic Association
1-800-986-4636
www.amerchiro.org

World Chiropractic Alliance
1-800-347-1011
www.worldchiropracticalliance.org

Headache

National Headache Foundation
1-800-643-5552
www.headaches.org

Holistic Medicine

American Holistic Medical Association
703-556-8729 (fax)
www.holisticmedicine.org

American Holistic Health Association
714-779-6152
www.ahha.org

Homeopathy

North American Society of Homeopaths
206-720-7000
www.homeopathy.org

Menopause

North American Menopause Society
440-442-7550
www.menopause.org

Naturopathy

American Association of Naturopathic Physicians
703-610-9037
www.naturopathic.org

Osteoporosis Prevention

National Osteoporosis Foundation
202-223-2226
www.nof.org

Stress Reduction

American Institute of Stress
914-963-1200
www.stress.org

International Stress Management Association
817-272-3869
www.stress-management-isma.org

Women's Health

MIOTI, Professional referrals on the Web
www.mioti.com

National Women's Health Network
202-347-1140 or 202-628-7814
www.nationalwomenshealthnetwork.org

References

The information in this book was compiled from sources selected because of the extensive medical documentation they provide. You may want to review these sources or read the actual medical reports referred to in these books or publications. Medical reports referenced in these sources may be obtained at medical libraries, in some public libraries, and on the Web.

ALTMAN, NAT. *Everybody's Guide to Chiropractic Health Care.* Los Angeles: J.P. Tarcher, 1990.

AMERICAN MEDICAL ASSOCIATION. *Essential Guide to Menopause.* New York: Pocket Books, 1998.

BUDOFF, PENNY WISE, M.D. *No More Hot Flashes and Other Good News.* New York: Warner Books, 1989.

CUTLER, WINNIFRED B., and C-R. GARCIA. *Menopause: A Guide for Women and the Men Who Love Them.* New York: W. W. Norton and Co., 1992.

DORESS, PAULA B., and DIANE L. SIEGAL, eds. *Ourselves Growing Older.* New York: Simon & Schuster, 1987.

Fletcher, Suzanne W., M.D., and Graham A. Colditz, M.D. "Failure of Estrogen Plus Progestin Therapy for Prevention." *Journal of the American Medical Association* 288 (July 17, 2002): 366–68.

Follingstad, A. H. "Estriol, the Forgotten Estrogen?" *Journal of the American Medical Association* 239 (January 2, 1978): 29–30.

Ford, Gillian. *What's Wrong with My Hormones?* Newcastle, Calif.: D. Ford Publications, 1992.

Frisch, Melvin, M.D. *Stay Cool Through Menopause.* New York: The Body Press/Perigee Books, 1993.

Gaby, Alan R., M.D. *Preventing and Reversing Osteoporosis.* Rocklin, Calif.: Prima Publishing, 1994.

Gittleman, Ann Louise. *Super Nutrition for Menopause.* New York: Pocket Books, 1993.

Greenwood, Sadja. *Menopause Naturally: Preparing for the Second Half of Life.* Volcano, Calif.: Volcano Press, 1992.

Harvard Women's Health Watch. Monthly newsletter available from Harvard Health Publications, 10 Shattuck St., Suite 612, Boston, Mass. 02115.
www.health.harvard.com

Henkel, Gretchen. *Making the Estrogen Decision.* Los Angeles: Lowell House, 1992.

Kamen, Betty. *Hormone Replacement Therapy, Yes or No?* Novato, Calif.: Nutrition Encounter, Inc., 1993.

Kastner, Mark, and Hugh Burroughs. *Alternative Healing: The Complete A–Z Guide to Over 160 Different Alternative Therapies.* Halcyon, Calif.: Halcyon Book Concern, 1993.

Lad, Vasant. *Ayurveda: The Science of Self-Healing, A Practical Guide.* Santa Fe, N. Mex.: Lotus Press, 1985.

LAVABRE, MARCEL F. *Aromatherapy Workbook*. Rochester, Vt.: Healing Arts Press, 1990.

LEE, JOHN R., M.D., JESSE HANLEY, M.D. *What Your Doctor May Not Tell You About Premenopause*. New York: Warner Books, 1999.

———, with VIRGINIA HOPKINS. *What Your Doctor May Not Tell You About Menopause*. New York: Warner Books, 1999.

LEMON, H. M. "Reduced Estriol Excretion in Patients with Breast Cancer Prior to Endocrine Therapy," *Journal of the American Medical Association* 196:(1966), 112–20.

LOCKIE, ANDREW. *The Women's Guide to Homeopathy: The Natural Way to a Healthier Life for Women*. New York: St. Martins Press, 1994.

MCCAIN, MARIAN VAN EYK. *Transformation Through Menopause*. New York: Bergen and Garvey, 1991.

MINDELL, EARL. *Earl Mindell's Vitamin Bible*. New York: Warner Books, 1991.

MURRAY, MICHAEL T. *The Healing Power of Herbs*. Rocklin, Calif.: Prima Publishing, 1992.

NISSIM, RINA. *Natural Healing in Gynecology*. New York: Pandora Press, 1986.

PERRY, SUSAN, and KATHERINE O'HANLAN, M.D. *Natural Menopause: The Complete Guide to a Woman's Most Misunderstood Passage*. New York: Addison-Wesley, 1992.

REITZ, ROSETTA. *Menopause—A Positive Approach*. New York: Random House, 1992.

SALAMAN, MAUREEN. *Foods That Heal*. Menlo Park, Calif.: MKS, Inc., 1994.

SMITH, TREVOR, M.D. *Homeopathic Medicine for Women, An Alternative Approach to Gynecological Health Care*. Rochester, Vt: Healing Arts Press, 1989.

STEIN, DIANE. *The Natural Remedy Book for Women.* Freedom, Calif.: Crossing Press, 1992.

STEWART, FELICIA, M.D., FELICIA GUEST, ET AL. *My Body, My Health: The Concerned Woman's Guide to Gynecology.* New York: John Wiley and Sons, 1979.

UTIAN, WULF H., and RUTH JACOBOWITZ. *Managing Your Menopause.* New York: Simon and Schuster/Fireside Press, 1992.

WAGNER, EDWARD M., M.D., and SYLVIA GOLDFARB. *How to Stay Out of the Doctor's Office: An Encyclopedia for Alternative Healing.* New York: Instant Improvement, Inc., 1992.

WARGA, CLAIRE L. PH.D. *Menopause and the Mind: The Complete Guide to Coping with Cognitive Effects of Perimenopause and Menopause, Including Memory Loss, Foggy Thinking, Verbal Confusion, and Verbal Slips.* New York: Touchstone Books, 2000.

WEIL, ANDREW. *Health and Healing: Understanding Conventional and Alternative Medicine.* Boston: Houghton Mifflin, 1983.

WHITAKER, JULIAN, M.D. *Health and Healing* (monthly newsletter). Available from Doctor-Proven Health Solutions, 7811 Montrose Road, Potomac, Md. 20854.

WOMEN'S HEALTH INITIATIVE. Web site www.nhlbi.nih.gov (August, 2002).

WOMEN'S HEALTH INITIATIVE, Writing Group for the Investigators. "Risks and Benefits of Estrogen Plus Progestin in Healthy Postmenopausal Women." *Journal of the American Medical Association* 288, no. 3, (July 17, 2002).